GETTING
MARRIED

WHEN IT'S NOT YOUR FIRST TIME

GETTING MARRIED

WHEN IT'S NOT YOUR FIRST TIME

*An Etiquette Guide
and Wedding Planner*

Pamela Hill Nettleton

Quill
An Imprint of HarperCollinsPublishers

HarperCollins books may be purchased for educational, business, or sales promotional use. For information please write: Special Markets Department, HarperCollins Publishers Inc., 10 East 53rd Street, New York, NY 10022.

FIRST EDITION

Designed by Nicola Ferguson

Library of Congress Cataloging-in-Publication Data
Nettleton, Pamela Hill.
Getting married when it's not your first time : an etiquette guide and wedding planner / by Pamela Hill Nettleton.—1st ed.
p.   cm.
ISBN 0-380-81077-8
1. Weddings—Planning.   2. Wedding etiquette.
3. Remarriage.   I. Title.
HQ745 .N47 2001
395.2'2—dc21   00-45915

01 02 03 04 05 ❖ RRD 10 9 8 7 6 5 4 3 2 1

CONTENTS

ACKNOWLEDGMENTS

Obviously, I could never have written this book without having three ex-husbands, and so I thank them: for life lessons; for friendship; and for, most wonderfully, our children. My fourth, final, and most fabulous husband, William Schrickel, has been a model of sincere and caring stepfathering, and I've paid attention and shared his insight here. I owe any real wisdom I possess to the best teachers and favorite people in my life: my three children, Gretchen Nettleton, Christopher Nettleton, and Ian Anderson. I thank them for patiently sharing their mother with a computer keyboard most evenings.

My research and work was supported by many local and national family therapists, psychologists, psychiatrists, counselors, and professionals who generously shared their experience and advice for parents and newly-re-weds. Among them are Judy Girard, Cecilia Soares, and Shirley Glass, Ph.D.

I cannot name individually but extend warm thanks to the countless single parents, stepparents, and stepchildren who spoke openly and candidly to me in phone, Internet, and personal interviews over the past several years. You are reinventing the American family, and you are doing it with love.

INTRODUCTION

So you're headed back to the altar. Congratulations!

Today, the stepfamily is the average American family. Second and third marriages have become so common that middle-aged adults now attend more remarriages of their friends than first marriages of their friends' children. These days, second weddings are often more sophisticated, individual, realistic, and romantic than first-time weddings because they are all about people who still believe firmly in love even after that belief has been sorely tested.

But second weddings are also complicated by a paralyzing number of complicated situations and concerns: ex-in-laws, children of the bride or groom, stepchildren, ex-stepchildren, divorced parents, and family and friends who were guests at the first wedding. Details and traditions can be unimaginably sticky, venturing into territory not addressed by most wedding guidebooks.

The trickiest bit of etiquette some brides face is how to word a formal, printed engagement announcement. Gasp! That *is* tricky. But how about real life? What do you do when your children from your first marriage want to be in your wedding party, but refuse to stand at the altar with his children? What's your action plan if your ex is threatening to appear at the church or temple? What the heck does a 40-year-old second-time bride wear for her wedding? What should her mother wear? And what if his children want to wear tuxedos and yours prefer tennis shoes?

The sometimes gritty, often hilarious real-life questions faced by encore brides and grooms are what this wedding guidebook is all about.

I've been married more times than you, almost certainly. I'm in my fourth (and very wonderful) marriage, and I'm raising three children from two marriages with a man who was divorced twice. So I know what you're going through, planning that second, third, or double-digit wedding. I've been married in a big church wedding with an enormous guest list. I've been married in a small church wedding with a few friends. I've been married in a hotel ballroom and in a restaurant dining room. I've been married by a priest, a minister, a New Age preacher, and a Jewish judge. I married a never-before-married man, a divorced man, a twice-divorced man, and a widower. I've been a stepmother and I've married stepfathers. I have made peace with in-laws and exes. My second husband played the trumpet at my first wedding, and my first husband and I attended my second husband's first wedding and knew his bride, who later became my husband's ex-wife and stepdaughter's mother. Never mind—that one confuses even me.

But I'm here to tell you that the rewards of marrying again and of blending families are great.

This guidebook will help you through what lies ahead with useful information from experienced wedding planners, guidance from family and stepfamily therapists, ideas from couples who have lived through all this and survived, and plain talk from the *real* experts—stepchildren.

So get yourself a pencil and put your feet up. This is going to be fun!

This book is organized into chapters in the order in which you're most likely to need them.

Within each chapter are worksheets that apply to the chapter's particular topic. Whenever you have a vendor to interview, a service to contract, or a big decision to make, there's a worksheet designed to help you through that experience with a list of common questions and spaces to write in your answers.

The last chapter is a comprehensive checklist of just about anything you need to prepare for your wedding.

Scattered through the chapters are quotes from other brides and grooms, advice from children of these couples, tips from experienced brides, and do's and don'ts that can help you through the coming months. There are also etiquette notes—with a difference. Few of us live in the rarefied social world that many etiquette tomes seem to address. Etiquette advice that just doesn't hold up in the real world doesn't appear in this book. The etiquette advice in this book is realistic and aimed at you—the encore bride.

A few matters of language

- ❖ Because many second-time brides and grooms have children, many of the suggestions and planning steps in this book include children. Rather than say, "if you have children," over and over again, I've usually skipped this phrase. If you do not have children, please do not feel excluded or overlooked!

- The words "church or temple" are used to represent all the types of religious sites you may choose for your wedding.

- The word "celebrant" is used to represent all the types of officials who celebrate a wedding: a priest, minister, rabbi, judge, pastor, chaplain, and so forth.

- The phrase "your children" includes both your children and your future stepchildren.

- Chances are, if you purchased this book and are reading it, you're a woman. So the language throughout is directed to you, but the information, help, and guidance are meant for both you and your fiancé, especially the information about supporting your children during this transition and about how to survive in a stepfamily.

GETTING
MARRIED

WHEN IT'S NOT YOUR FIRST TIME

CHAPTER ONE

YOUR BIGGEST WORRIES ABOUT MARRYING AGAIN

Life is just full of surprises, isn't it?

Do you remember a time when you were sure you could never feel this way again? And now, here you are—as happy as a teenager.

Congratulations!

Now, what are you worrying about?

Worries About Marrying Again

"*I'm too old to be a bride!*"

No, you're not. Once upon a time, the average age of a bride was 18 or 19. Today, it's 26 or 27 and getting older all the time.

Why? It's true that many people are getting married for

the first time at a later stage in their lives. But the number of second marriages is also rising, and third and fourth marriages are no longer rarities that occur only in Hollywood. More than 30 percent of weddings today involve at least one partner who was married before.

Second weddings are hot. Second weddings are more sophisticated, cooler, funkier, more fun. They are more shamelessly romantic, in the way only two people who already know what a 3 A.M. feeding is like can be.

You, my dear, are not alone.

"The bridal salon consultant will laugh at me!"

No, she won't. Bridal salons, ring designers, florists, caterers, and dress designers have noticed that you are one of a swiftly multiplying number of women: encore brides. They are reconfiguring their businesses to appeal to you. A 40-year-old is not an uncommon sight in a bridal salon, nor is a 50- or 60-year-old. And if you're 70, honey, bless your heart.

"What will people (my children, my ex, my family, my friends) think?"

Your children and your future stepchildren will need extra love and support from both you and your fiancé. Tips, guidance, and advice from both stepparents and stepchildren are offered in the chapters to come.

Your ex-spouse could be a little irritant or a big problem, but if he was supportive of you and your choices, he wouldn't *be* your ex, now, would he? The next chapter is devoted to how to deal with him and how to deal with your fiancé's ex, too.

If your husband died, you may be worried about what his parents and family will think. There's advice ahead for you, as well.

Your parents and siblings, I hope, have your best interests at heart and will share your joy and happiness.

Your friends are probably reminding you that you stormed around for months after your divorce, swearing you'd *never* walk down the aisle again. They may be a little jealous. After all, you've found love all over again. Lucky you!

"What if I fail again?"

Well, you've changed. Remember that you have a tremendous advantage now that you didn't have the last time you thought about marriage: You are older, wiser, and more experienced. You've survived the end of a major love partnership. You've lost love and regained it. You can use what you've learned to create a new, lasting relationship. Your new marriage can be anything you two make it. You have the strengths you each developed in your previous relationships, and you have the new combined strengths you've developed together.

Congratulations!

Do You Deserve Another Real Wedding?

Not too many etiquette manuals ago, a second wedding was barely an occasion at all. It was a subdued affair, attended only by immediate family and treated as quietly as possible.

Not anymore! Today, a second wedding is celebrated as joyfully as a first—even more so because it is a joining of a more mature bride and groom who have a deeper understanding of their vows and who have triumphed over personal challenges.

> ## HOW WE DID IT
> There is nothing wrong with keeping on trying. I don't feel foolish because I took a chance on love. Hey, I'm alive and I'm trying to really live my life! That's more than lots of people do.
> —*Elsa, 57*

You have to be brave to try again, and you and your fiancé have not only tried, but succeeded!

A second or third commitment to marriage doesn't mean it's less of a commitment. Marriage is a significant, life-changing event, whenever it occurs, and deserves to be marked with importance and ceremony.

This Wedding Will Be Special in Its Own Ways

You and your fiancé have already learned that love is unique. Your new marriage will be inherently different from your first in many ways. Your wedding should be, too.

Don't create a rerun of your first wedding. Start fresh. Start over. Find new ways to celebrate.

Do not, under any circumstances, get married in the same church or temple, hotel, or park as one of you did the first time around. Do not use the same ring, choose the same celebrant, embrace the same color scheme. Do not honeymoon on the same island. And you already know better than to wear the same dress. Create your wedding out of the unique style that you and your fiancé make together. Make new memories, rather than relive old ones.

Stop Being Embarrassed and Have Fun

My husband (yes, he's my fourth) and I (I'm his third) did a silly thing at a party the night before our wedding that helped keep things lighthearted. We ordered a wedding cake from an earnest baker who had no idea what we were about to do to his carefully sculpted tiers and flourishes. We stuck a bride and groom on top, but then added little extra plastic people. Two previous brides for him, three ex-tuxedoes for me. They tumbled down the sides and layers of the cake, heads mashed into frosting, miniature dress shoes and tiny plastic hoop skirts sticking out awkwardly. We did check with the kids first to be sure they wouldn't be offended by seeing their parents in effigy in frosting. Cake therapy.

Actually, it was kind of fun, and it set people at ease. Everyone knew, of course, that we had been married before, but sometimes people treat it like an unfortunate flaw that shouldn't be brought up. Well, we brought it up and then some, everyone got a chuckle, and the cake wasn't bad, either.

My husband also produced a wedding napkin that I forbade him to use at our wedding (it became a rehearsal dinner feature, instead). He used the "no smoking" symbol of a circle with a slash through it, removed the cigarette, and replaced it with the names of our past relationships. One side of the napkin held three circles with slashes: "Pam and Jeff" (my first), "Pam and Mike" (my second), "Pam and Len" (my third). His past loves were circled and slashed on the other side of the napkin. And in the middle, "Pam and Bill—together at last!" My husband's sense of humor may seem a bit oddball, but he's not far off base. We survive life's challenges best if we learn to laugh at ourselves.

> **HOW WE DID IT**
> We only had one rule for ourselves. This time, we did what we wanted.
> —*David, 43*

So laugh. Enjoy. Have fun. There aren't *that* many times in our lives when we can buy those bridal magazines. So go out there and do all that fun girl stuff—indulge your Barbie doll side. Window shop for rings. Daydream about honeymoons. Pore over pictures of dresses. Feel like a bride. You are one.

Please Yourself

First-time brides worry about pleasing mothers-in-law, college roommates, the Vanderbilts, and the Posts. This is how they end up wearing dresses their best friends picked out, standing next to thirteen bridesmaids wrapped in puce, listening to the dreadful song stylings of their cousin, Drucilla. An encore bride knows that bouquet ribbons dyed to match ballroom carpeting don't guarantee a long-lasting partnership. Now that you've had a life for a while, you and your fiancé can codesign a wedding and marriage to reflect and support it.

If you always wanted a big church or temple wedding but didn't get one the first time, do it now. If you wanted your first wedding to be elegant and intimate but had to have an enormous chicken salad buffet reception for 500 the first time, do what *you* want the second time.

Throw a Great Party

Some folks sweep second weddings under the rug, acting like they aren't really nuptials, sizing them down into something like a slightly dressed-up family picnic. Oh, for Pete's sake, celebrate. You're older now. You have friends who've known you a good decade or two and who have seen you through some rough times. There are precious few excuses in life to gather everyone who loves you into one room for a day. Enjoy it.

❧ Tip ❧

Do share planning responsibilities with your fiancé. Chances are that your mother isn't helping much—or *as* much—this time around. Don't shoulder everything yourself.

❧ Etiquette Notes ❧

❧ If you have silver with your old monogram on it, keep it. It's too valuable to replace, and heirloom silver can be passed down, regardless of the initials.

- If you were divorced, your new monogram is your first-name initial, your husband's last-name initial, if you take his name, and your maiden-name initial. If you were widowed, your new monogram is your first-name initial, your new husband's last-name initial, and your first husband's last-name initial or your maiden-name initial.

- If you have quality linens with your old monogram, you may wish to save them for a daughter, use them in a guest room, or simply store them—in time, your new husband may feel comfortable using them.

Ms. Nomer: What Are You Going to Call Yourself?

Before your wedding

"I've been married before" covers your situation for most folks, but you'll notice that bridal salons, magazines, and media have begun to struggle with this increasingly common situation that seems to be sans adjective. "Encore bride" is one of my personal favorites. It's certainly better than "faded flower," "tarnished tulip," and "repeat offender," anyway.

❧ Kids Talk ❧

I was really upset when my mom gave up my dad's name when she got married. In a way, it made me feel sort of like an orphan. Like I didn't have any parents with my same name who were still alive.

—*Todd, 10*

After your wedding

Traditionally, a first-time bride adds her new husband's name to her own. She may use her maiden name in signatures and legal matters, may use it as a sort of hyphenated name without the hyphen, or may even legally hyphenate her name with his, giving them each a new last name.

If you were married only briefly before or kept your maiden name, you probably won't confuse people whatever name you choose this time. However, if you were married for a long time after you took your first husband's name and have kept his name after your divorce or his death, changing your name now may present some special problems. Family and friends may literally not recognize your name for a while. Your last name will be different from your children's. (It doesn't sound like a big issue until you have to write explanations in the margins of school forms and argue with the school nurse that yes, you really are Tommy's mother and she should let you take him home.) And if you've built up a work reputation linked to your name, changing it now may even hurt you professionally.

Your decision about how to change—or not change—your name is a personal one. Changing your name at 18 is not as major a life change as changing your name at 42 or 55 or 60. You'll want to consider how a change may affect your children, family, friends, colleagues, and business clients. You'll want to talk to your fiancé about his feelings.

If you do add your new husband's name to yours, you may wish to retain—legally or informally—your previous maiden or married name when it would help clarify matters. For example, suddenly signing your name "Katherine Woodson" when everyone has known you as "Katherine O'Hara" may cause real problems. "Katherine O'Hara Wood-

My maiden name was Pamela Hill. When I first married at 18, I added my husband's name: Pamela Hill Nettleton. After our divorce, I kept that name because it was my children's last name. I was also building a career as a writer, and I didn't want to lose whatever name recognition with editors and readers that I had managed to build by that point. When I remarried, I considered taking my husband's name, but the professional concern was even more of an issue after more years as "Pamela Hill Nettleton" had passed. And, his first wife's name had also been "Pam"—I didn't want to be Pam Anderson #2. When I married my third husband, he wanted me to take his name. I changed my business stationery to my first and his last name and tried to keep "Pamela Hill Nettleton" as my byline. That confused everyone. When I married again at 40, I kept "Pamela Hill Nettleton." It's who I've been since I was 18. It's the last name of two of my three children. It just feels like who I am. Although it may bother some husbands to have a wife with a last name from her first husband, a woman always has the last name of a man, even when it's her father. My husband understands, and I love him for it.

son" may be a good temporary solution or even a permanent choice.

A typical choice for a widow is to use her first name, her first husband's last name, and her new husband's last name: "Abigail Andrews Wingert." If you are divorced, but like this solution, borrow it.

It is also legal for you to have two names: one for your

professional use (your "stage name") and one for your personal and social use.

Prenuptial Agreements and Arguments

If you went through a difficult and messy divorce, you may be wondering if signing a prenuptial agreement now may prevent arguments and financial disaster later. Or your reasons may have little to do with a future divorce—you may just be looking for a tool to bring financial issues, wills, provisions for children, and other matters to the table. You are right to want to discuss these matters directly and clearly and to settle legal questions before your marriage takes place. Whether a prenuptial agreement is the right vehicle for doing so is up to you.

Meet with your attorney—and suggest that your fiancé meet with his—to discuss how prenuptial agreements work, what matters are usually included in one, and if one would be a good idea for you. Your attorney may have other suggestions for ways that you and your fiancé can resolve some of the complicated legal and financial matters of a blended family.

Your fiancé may not be fond of the idea of a prenuptial. He may take it as a sign of a lack of faith in your impending marriage or as predestining your union for failure. If your concern is primarily to protect your children (and his), he may find this topic easier to discuss.

If your fiancé is the one who suggested a prenuptial agreement, you may be wondering if it means he already has one foot out the door. This can be a difficult and sensitive issue. You'll want to speak frankly about it together—with an attorney, and possibly in a session with a therapist, just to have an objective third party.

❧ Don't ❧

Don't get paralyzed by "But I'm not a first-time bride!" thinking. Every couple deserves the fun, fuss, and romance of a wedding.

❧ Resources ❧

A company called Wedding Helpers produces a name-change kit that you may find helpful. Check out its web site at www.weddinghelpers.com or phone (800) 274–0675.

CHAPTER TWO

RECOVERING FROM THE EXES

(or from the Loss of Your Spouse)

You are about to begin an exciting new chapter in your life, but you have already lived through a few chapters that won't ever go away.

If your spouse died, you and your children have survived a devastating life experience. Surely, there was a time when you wondered if you would ever feel joy and happiness again. Now, you have found a new love. But every so often you notice a twinge or memory. Are these signs that you should not remarry?

If you've been through a divorce, especially a difficult one, you and your children have also been through a devastating life experience. To have a new joy to celebrate and share is wonderful. But you may have new worries, too. Will news of my wedding irritate my ex? Will my children adjust? Will this marriage end badly, too?

Such concerns and worries are not second thoughts about

your new marriage. They are simply the normal, natural feelings of anyone who has been through what you have.

If Your First Husband Died

In a way, saying hello to a new relationship and a new life with your fiancé is saying a final good-bye to your deceased spouse. You may be surprised to experience occasional waves of grief that you thought you had finally put behind you. These feelings are not necessarily signs that you should not go ahead with your engagement and wedding. More likely, they are a natural adjustment to the significant change in your life.

If you have children, understand that they will experience these sorts of feelings, too. If they receive the exciting news of your engagement with lukewarm enthusiasm, give them time. They may need a chance to absorb the idea and adjust to their new future. Let them know that you are also having special memories about their father at this time. Share a few stories with your children of happy memories of your first wedding. It will help you connect and help them imagine and understand your happiness now.

What to tell your previous in-laws

If your previous husband died, you and your children may have quite a close relationship with your in-laws. You may feel awkward about telling them that you have become engaged. This may feel like a posthumous rejection of their son, and you may feel as if you are being disloyal somehow. Understand if their initial reaction is understated or even negative. Be patient and give them time. As they experience kind treatment from you and your fiancé, they'll feel reassured that they are welcome to remain in the lives of their grandchildren.

❧ REMEMBER ❧

Your fiancé has his own previous relationships or marriage to "grieve" or say good-bye to, just like you do. Give him room and be patient.

New Marriage, Old Ex

Planning to remarry may seem like you've left your ex in the dust—but when you have children, your ex (and your fiancé's ex) have a way of hanging on. And on.

Your ex picks up your children for the weekend. His ex calls to arrange a school vacation trip for your stepchildren-to-be. Though your divorce is long final and you're head over heels in love with your fiancé, your relationship with your ex is one you will never completely shake. You and your ex are parents together, which means that, for better or worse, you'll have to tolerate—and sometimes even sit right next to—each other at band concerts and high school graduations.

You have a choice to make. You can fuss, complain, and throw a tantrum every time your ex tosses a monkey wrench into your plans, but only if you want to build your new marriage on a foundation of old resentment and convince your fiancé that you never quite got over your first husband. Or you can learn how to manage your relationship with your ex successfully, helping your children—and your new marriage—get off to a healthier start.

What to tell your ex-in-laws

Your relationship with your ex-in-laws may be over, so this may not be an option for you. But if your relationship is good, as it sometimes is when grandparents and grandchildren remain close, you should let them know your plans. Do so without saying anything negative or judgmental about their son. Make the news simple and direct. Imagine their main concern—probably that they'll still be able to see their grandchildren often—and reassure them about it.

Good Ex-etiquette

Don't try to like each other—just be polite

A big mistake that divorced couples make is to try to work things out between themselves. Hey, you couldn't do it when you were married to each other. What makes you think you can do it now that you're divorced? Don't try to resolve conflicts. Don't try to agree. Such attempts are probably doomed, anyway, and you'll only stir up ancient resentments. Instead, aim for amicable coexistence.

Extend to your ex the well-mannered civility you'd offer any business client (even one you don't like much). Don't be snide, don't be snippy, don't be mean. If you can't be warm, at least be polite. Say things like, "Hm. Guess we can't agree on that one. So, when are you picking the kids up on Thursday?"

This goes double if your kids are around and can overhear you. You do your children no big favors by being snotty to their dad, and you probably increase their stress level significantly.

Give yourself extra-credit points if you can actually manage to be kind ("Bobby got an A on his math test, and we wanted you to hear it first!") or thoughtful ("I know you have a business trip this weekend—would it help if I kept Bobby for an extra day?").

Your ex has only as much power as you give him

Sure, he can be irritating, and yes, he knows just how to push your buttons. But you and your ex don't live under the same roof any longer, and if his opinions rattle your cage, it's only because you're letting him do that to you.

Put your energy into your new relationship

My ex-husband went through an annoying period of calling me almost every day to complain about something. My daughter arrived at his house missing a mitten—what kind of mother was I? My son's pants were too short—was my life so busy that I couldn't buy him clothes that fit? One day, his new wife answered the phone, and I blurted out, "If I were you, I'd sure want my husband's energy going to his new marriage, not his old one."

She's a nice lady and forgave my rude comment. Then, she went to my ex and suggested that he reorder his priorities, putting his new marriage ahead of his old one. He did, and things have been much smoother ever since.

Trashing your ex isn't foreplay

When Louis and Rose met, they discovered they had something in common: disastrous first marriages. They became allies in the war of the exes, calling each other every time an ex misbehaved or an attorney sent a letter.

"We'd talk all night about how awful my ex-husband was and how deceitful his first wife was," says Rose. "We were good support for each other, but we weren't building anything new and fresh together."

Louis set a new rule: Complain about your old marriage for ten minutes, but talk about what's great about our new marriage for twenty. "That forced us out of our negative pattern into something really positive," says Louis. "Once Rose started to tell me some of the things she appreciated about me, I realized I had been missing that. Concentrating on what didn't work before almost kept us from building something positive together now."

Share your frustrations with your new husband, but don't let frustration be all you share. Mutual anger and resentment can form a powerful bond—but not a sexy or loving one.

Trashing his ex is self-destructive

You and your fiancé may have ex-relationships in common, but choose to focus your new relationship on building positive experiences together, rather than dwelling on your past pain.

Ramona and Burt were madly in love, but their biggest conflict was Burt's ex-wife. Whenever Sylvia's name came up, Ramona added a snide comment or insult to the conversation.

One day, Ramona realized that acting spiteful was endangering her new marriage. "Every nasty thing I said about Sylvia made *me* look like a shrew, not Sylvia!" says Ramona. "Now and then, I try to say something nice about Burt's ex. It doesn't make him run back to her—it makes him think I'm pretty terrific."

Don't compete with his ex for motherhood awards

Your first task as a stepmother: *relax*. His kids already have a mother; you don't have to fill that role. Instead, work to create a welcoming environment for his children in your home. Think of yourself as an extra adult in his children's lives. Come into your stepchildren's lives gently. Have fun. Play. Leave the disciplining to your husband and his ex.

❖ DO UNTO YOUR EX ❖

When your ex remarries, be kind and supportive. Say nothing snotty about his new wife to your children.

Telling Your Ex About Your Engagement

Tell your ex in person, if you can. This is important news that will affect your children for the rest of their lives and should be delivered personally.

If your relationship with your ex is difficult, you may dread this task. It may help to keep your message brief, direct, and clear. Your ex has probably been aware that you and your fiancé have been seeing each other for some time and may be somewhat prepared for this news.

Try something like: "Brad and I have decided to get married. We're thinking the wedding may be in about ten months or so—I'll let you know as soon as our plans are firm. I've told the children, and I expect they'll have mixed feelings. I'll keep talking to them, and I appreciate your support."

Your ex may feel that his place with his children is being usurped by your fiancé. Try to put this particular resentment to rest (and save yourself some grief) by reassuring him: "Brad and I have talked a lot about what his role with the children should be. You are their father, and Brad is not going to try to take your place in any way."

Even if your relationship with your ex is generally positive, you may be surprised at his reaction and your own mixed feelings. Although you think you're done grieving your divorce, a new wedding means that your previous marriage and partnership are truly gone—expect to feel some ambivalence (and expect to see it in the children, too).

If you have an ax-carrying ex

If you are unlucky enough to have an ex who is violent or unreasonable and fear that he'll crash your wedding, it may be wise to keep your wedding plans quiet for now. If you have no children, you don't need ever to tell him. If he rarely sees your children, you can let your children know your plans and proceed with them. But if he sees your children regularly, you can't ask your children to hide your news for you. In that case, let your children and your fiancé spend time together, but don't let your children know your wedding plans until shortly before the wedding. Set your date for a time when your children would normally be with you. Your ex can learn of your wedding only after the fact.

If one of your exes is threatening to crash your wedding and make a scene, it may be an attempt to intimidate you—but it may really happen. If you're very troubled by this possibility, consider obtaining a restraining order or hiring a security guard to monitor the wedding and reception. These steps may sound extreme, but if they guarantee you peace of mind on your big day, then they're worth it. You may also try to head off this scene ahead of time. Identify someone in the family to whom the ex will listen and ask that person to call on the ex and have a frank discussion.

HOW WE DID IT

We had to tell our exes about our engagement early, so that we were sure we could get our children for that weekend. That was the most important thing to us—we didn't want to start our wedding plans until we knew for sure that we could all be together. Teresa's ex-husband was cool, but my ex-wife was fairly snotty. "Are you sure you're ready to remarry?" Now that several years have passed, I realized that back then, my first wife felt pretty threatened about Teresa's involvement with our daughters. It was rough going with my ex for a while, but Teresa, and time, won her over.

—*Max, 33*

Let your children know that this behavior is not their fault and try not to discuss this situation in front of them.

❧ KIDS TALK ❧

My mom remarried when I was 12. I felt like I had to keep telling my dad that my new stepdad wouldn't take his place. I felt like if I got excited about my mom's wedding, my dad would get mad at me. For a while, it was pretty confusing. But my dad sent my mom a card after her wedding, wishing her luck and saying nice things. Mom showed it to me, and I felt better after that.

—*Clark, 15*

❧ Don't ❧

❧ Don't spoil the fun of your engagement by grousing about his ex or yours.

❧ Don't keep reminiscing about how perfect your first wedding (or first husband!) was.

❧ Don't obsess over your ex's response to your news. The feelings and needs of you, your children, and your fiancé come first.

❧ Don't invite your ex to your wedding. Even if your fiancé says he feels fine about it, you'll be creating an awkward situation for your children, your parents, and your guests.

❧ Etiquette Notes ❧

If you wish to invite your deceased spouse's parents and family to your wedding and your fiancé feels comfortable with this plan, do so.

If you, your fiancé, or your children seem to be "stuck" and focused on the past, consider scheduling either a family therapy session or a private therapy session to talk through what's going on. If the problem is severe, you may want to postpone your wedding date until things are more positive. Most likely, a chance to talk through concerns with a professional and objective third party will clear the air.

Many communities have support groups for blended families. A visit to such a group now may help you head off future problems before they become entrenched. Call your community hospital or help line to find a group near you.

If you'd like help breaking this news to you ex, many communities offer mediation services through the court system. Ask if you are eligible to have a mediator present when you speak with your ex. A third party can be of great help. You may be asked to pay a modest fee.

CHAPTER THREE

ANNOUNCING YOUR ENGAGEMENT

Chances are, this second time around, your engagement was less of a question-and-answer event and more of a gradual, joint decision. You two have probably been considering this step for some time and may have spoken to your children about the possibility.

But now, it's more than a possibility—it's a reality. How you announce your intentions to your children and your family can help you make your future as loving and successful as it can be.

Telling Your Children

Stop! Your first urge may be to grab the phone, call up your best friend, and scream your good news. Don't do it! Before you make a move, consider who needs to know first.

If you and/or your fiancé have children, they must be your first priority. It is not an exaggeration to say that it can be disastrous to let your children and stepchildren learn about their future in secondhand conversation. Letting your children know first tells them that you put them first. Letting them find out from others can make them feel like pawns with no control or input over their own lives—and can create resentment just when you're trying to build loving cooperation.

Explaining mushy stuff

Dating, getting engaged, and acting romantic in front of our children makes us self-conscious. That's why our parents got it over with long before most of us ever showed up. But this

Who needs to know?	How should you tell them?
1. Your children and your fiancé's children	In person
2. If you have grandchildren, your grandchildren	In person
3. Your parents and your fiancé's parents	In person
4. Your exes	In person or by phone and before the children go visit dad and spill the beans
5. Your friends	In person, by phone, or by letter (they'll spread the word!)

is more than just romance—this is a big event in your life, and you share big life events with your children. You have an opportunity here to model big-life-event behavior for your children. And this particular event will change your children's lives profoundly. Don't brush this off as grown-up stuff that the kids don't need to talk about. They are in the center of the action, and you should treat them accordingly.

Honey, meet the kids

If your children have never met your fiancé, then you *must* halt your engagement and wedding plans and take time to introduce your new family to each other before you make your engagement public. If your children are still living with you and are school-aged or younger, plan to devote several months to slowly introducing your fiancé to them and them to him—without any talk of marriage. If your children are older and living on their own, a shorter period may be fine—but you may be surprised at how strong a reaction older children can have to Mom or Dad remarrying.

Children need a "first date," too. You got to know your new love over time, with repeated meetings and encounters that eventually grew into dates and a relationship. Don't plop your kids into an intimate family scene (like introducing them to Bob and then announcing that he's their new daddy) and expect them to embrace Bob warmly. That's a recipe for disaster.

Here's a recipe for success: Choose neutral turf, like a restaurant. Meet your fiancé there. Drive your children, so there is private time to talk, coming and going. Set a half-hour limit: hello, let's have dessert, gotta run. Do not touch, kiss, or even sit next to your fiancé. Do not talk about marriage. And no lingering glances or endearing nicknames, either. A simple kiss can be quite upsetting to a child, especially if dad's death or the divorce wasn't all that long ago. (And even if the end of your first marriage—whatever the nature of it—was a long time ago, children almost always harbor secret hopes of reconciliation or of Dad miraculously re-

turning.) Be affectionate all you want in private, but when the kids are around, take it s-l-o-w-l-y. It's a long-range investment that will pay off with your children being more accepting and less feisty.

What loss feels like to a child

To a child, dating and remarriage feel like loss.

Let's count the losses to a child when divorce or death occurs:

- Loss of the parent who died or the parent "lost" in the divorce

- Loss of the familiar home, school, neighborhood, and friends if a move occurred

- Loss of innocence: "Now I know people can die or leave."

- Loss of the child's idea of what a family is: "Now I belong to a family with a different shape and size."

- Loss of feeling normal

- Loss of feeling safe

Now, add the losses that occur when Mom starts dating again:

- Loss of the hope and fantasy that Mom and Dad will get back together again

- Loss of having Mom "to myself"

- Loss of the new family just created; now things are different again.

And, the losses when Mom remarries:

- Loss of time alone with Mom

- Loss of feeling at home with my family: "Now I live with a stranger."

- Loss of privacy

- Loss of the familiar home, school, neighborhood, and friends if a move occurs

Though an engagement and wedding plans are exciting undertakings for you, remember they are fraught with loss for your children. Even if your children understand why you are divorced or have been supported through their grief of losing a parent, the presence of your fiancé turns a glaring floodlight on the cold, hard fact that their family, as they knew and loved it, is gone. Your children may see your fiancé as competition, no matter how carefully and tenderly you explain to them that you will always love them, that they will always be your children, that your relationship with them will never go away. (By the way, be sure that you *do* explain this to them—many times.)

Children can be saboteurs, and who can blame them? They're not trying to ruin your life—they are trying to protect their own. You, as an adult, can visualize the future. They, as children, cannot. They only know the past. And they liked the past.

Cecelia Soares, a marriage and family therapist and seminar speaker based in California, says, "A parent remarrying is the death of a little flame that children carry. Even as adults, they don't give up that fantasy that Mom and Dad will get back together again. I wish more people realized that fact because they'd change how they spoke to their children about a new relationship."

Why Focusing on Your Children Helps Them—and Your Marriage

The loss of the fantasy

Children tenaciously cling to the fantasy that their divorced parents will get back together again. When you start to date, and certainly if you remarry, this fantasy is dashed.

Judy Girard is a licensed marriage and family therapist, an executive faculty member of the Colorado School of Professional Psychology in Colorado Springs, Colorado, and the clinic director of the Switzer Counseling Center. Judges refer difficult divorce mediation cases to Girard, who specializes in working with families, stepfamilies, and children of divorce.

Girard tells the story of her own second wedding day, ten years after her divorce, when her 21-year-old daughter confessed, "I always thought you and Dad would get back together again." Girard says, "You could have knocked me over with a feather! What?! What?! How could she *possibly* have thought that? Her father and I are amicable, we attend functions together, but no way were there ever any signals that we might get back together. Children, all the way into adulthood, probably *never* give up that fantasy that Mom and Dad will get back together."

Children's fantasies of a perfect mom-dad-children household may actually work to your advantage. When I remarried, my grade school-aged child said, "Good. Now we're a family." I was shocked. Surely, we had been a family all those years when it was just me at the helm of the household. Was our family suddenly more legitimate now that a man was moving in? Well, yes—sometimes, in some children's eyes.

Even if your children don't embrace the idea of a new man around the house, your understanding of their fantasy that their parents will get back together is important. Be gentle with your children's balkiness and recognize that it may signal a form of grief. Give your children time to adjust to the loss of their old hopes and the arrival of a new family member. Lower your expectations that your children will welcome the new guy with open arms—in fact, lower those expectations to zero. By relieving your children of that pressure, you are helping them adjust to reality at their own pace.

If your children are grown

If your children are grown, you don't need to spoon-feed them (they'll probably figure out that if you're introducing them to a guy, he may be "the One"), but you do need to respect them. Put yourself in their place. They've come through some hard times of grieving your first marriage with you, and they've grown into a single-parent family with you. Now, you're adding a new person into *their* family system, and they don't even get a vote. Will you ever have time alone for them again? Will things ever be even somewhat the way they used to be? Will you be moving? Will their roots, already transplanted once, have to shift again?

Your children love you and want you to be happy, but you should try to realize that they will be experiencing a complex and confusing rush of emotions that they themselves may not immediately understand. You probably didn't believe you could ever love again, and the idea may have grown on you gradually. Give your children time (just the thing couples in love don't want to wait for!).

Here's a hint: Read through the suggestions here for younger children. Though your children are grown, their feelings can still be quite childlike when it comes to how they feel about you. Your understanding of what they are going through can help you react to and support them in loving ways that help all of you.

Ways to help older children adjust to your remarriage

+ Find opportunities for just you to spend time with them—don't include your fiancé in all family activities for a while.

+ Try to imagine what your grown children's concerns about your remarriage are and address them. If they're worried about financial matters, have a frank discussion about what you've arranged. As soon as they realize that you haven't cut them out of your will and that their mother's belongings will still go to them, you may have some strong supporters for your new happiness.

+ Don't punish your children for speaking their minds. Invite them to tell you how they feel and don't punish them when they do it. Listen without ranting back.

If your children are young

Don't wait until you and your fiancé have made all your decisions for the future before you let your children in on them. Your children will want to know where you're going to live, when the wedding will happen, and more things that you may not yet know the answers to. But tell them you are thinking about their questions and that their opinion is important to you. If you're looking for a new house, let them know that you're looking for one with a backyard big enough for a baseball game and bedrooms big enough for their goalie equipment. Let them know they'll be involved as soon as the time is right.

There is no set length of time that your engagement must last. The more complex your wedding plans, the more time you'll need to prepare. The most important issue in setting your wedding date is how your children and your future stepchildren are adjusting. If you can give them some months to get used to the idea now, you will likely reap benefits later.

Ways to help younger children adjust to your remarriage

❖ Don't tell your children to stop talking about when Dad died or to stop bringing up the divorce. To your children, your engagement now and what they lost in your first marriage are interconnected. Let them talk about it all, mixed up together.

❖ Don't shame your children or make them feel wrong for continuing to grieve while you feel ready to date again. Remember when you needed unconditional support and acceptance from friends and family? Extend that support and acceptance to your children.

❖ Don't talk about this once and think you're done. Bring it up again and again.

❖ Don't take silence for acceptance. If your children don't ask questions, ask questions for them. "Say, I bet you were wondering about . . ." Jump-start the conversation.

❖ Do display rays of hope: "I know this adjustment is hard now, but if we keep talking and hugging, it's going to get better." "I know you've been through a lot of changes, but things won't always be this confusing." "This is making you feel really sad about Dad, but it won't always make us sad to think of him."

- ❖ Do repeat the same messages over and over. Your children's ability to understand keeps changing, so keep sending messages. And, even if your children hear "the divorce wasn't your fault," they probably need to hear it repeatedly before it sinks into their hearts.

- ❖ Do accept what your children say. Even if it's at top decibel and far from tactful, don't shut down communication with a punishing message. Manage at least a "Wow! You really feel strongly about that! You've given me a lot to think about. Can we talk about this again tomorrow?"

What creates anxiety for children differs from what creates anxiety for adults. Try to think like a child and be prepared to answer your children's questions.

- ❖ Will I have to change schools?
- ❖ Will I have to share a room?
- ❖ If we move to his house, is it cooler than ours?
- ❖ Do I have to put up with his kids?
- ❖ Will I still see my dad?
- ❖ Will Dad be mad?
- ❖ Will I lose my friends?

* Do I have to mind him?

* Does he have dumb rules?

Realize that everyone in your family will be making adjustments over the coming weeks and years. Yes, years. So keep talking together about each other's adjustments. Let your children know that you understand they are getting used to a new stepdad. Let your stepchildren know that you understand they are getting used to a new stepmom. Let your fiancé know that you understand he is getting used to a new family and wife. If this sounds like you are doing most of the work, you're catching on. So come back as a man next time. What can I tell you?

❖ KIDS TALK ❖

A guy who says, "Hey, Junior! Hey, Sport! Hey, Tiger! Hey, Slick!" I could not respect a person like that.
—*Ian, 13*

Listen, listen, listen

Whatever the age of your children, when you tell them about your engagement, you must prepare yourself to be a listener, not a teller. Although you are making an announcement, what you are really there for is to listen to their reactions and to let them know that you are willing to hear them out. If you listen well, without anger, you have just laid the groundwork for a positive relationship between your fiancé and your children.

Your children may even worry that if they tell you what they think of your fiancé, you'll hate them. Or you'll leave them. Or you'll give them back to Daddy full time and take off with your new husband. It will help them immeasurably if you simply allow them to speak to you about their feelings.

First, imagine the things your children might possibly say that would hurt you or make you panic the most. "You love your boyfriend more than you love us!" "Can't you marry Dad again?" "You're a terrible mother!"

Then, picture yourself "hearing" these feelings without clenching up and reacting negatively. You want to show your children that no matter how scary their feelings sound, you are willing to listen to them.

If your child won't open up, try expressing the feelings you think he or she may be having. Try "I was thinking that when we're all together with Bob, that could make you miss Dad a lot," "You had fun with Bob and me today. I was thinking that you may feel guilty about that, like you were cheating on Daddy by liking Bob," or "When Bob takes us all to the movies, you probably remember when Dad used to do that."

As your child hears her most terrible feelings spoken out loud by you and sees you remaining calm and loving toward her, she may have a strong reaction. You may get, as I once did, a sudden, shuddering sob and a child throwing himself into your lap for a hug and a good, long cry. You may also get, as I also once did, a shrug, a sigh, and a "Do whatever you want, Mom—I love you."

Another good way to get your children to talk is to tell them about your feelings. Plenty is going on with you. Share some of it. But—and this is a big *but*—remember that you are the parent. Don't expect your children to be your peer support system. You support each other as a family, but your children should not have to support you as though they were your best friends. They deserve your protection, and they need to know you are the adult.

Making the announcement

◆ Make your announcement in person. You can't see your child's reaction on the phone. This news is important enough to deliver face-to-face.

◆ Talk to each child separately, so each can express his or her feelings without being influenced by siblings. Also, this can help you "take the temperature" of each child and really understand what each is feeling. If you talk to all the children at once, the quiet one will seem acquiescent, but may surprise you later with a temper tantrum.

◆ Talk to each child on the same day. If you tell one child the news a week before you tell your other child, you've just added gasoline to the sibling-rivalry fire.

◆ Leave your fiancé at home. Don't bring your fiancé along for this announcement. This talk is between you and your children. Your fiancé should do the same for his children.

◆ Don't rush it. Allow enough time for your children to ask questions. Plan a lunch with time to take a walk and talk afterward or tell them at the beginning of a weekend when you'll all be together for a few days.

◆ Be willing to witness and allow room for a wide range of feelings.

✦ Don't assume one grand announcement takes care of things. Keep asking your children how they are feeling in the grocery store, on the way home from school, in the car going to hockey. Keep probing for feelings or just announce yours now and then. "Boy, all this wedding planning sure is exhausting! I'm missing my quiet time with you playing checkers!"

Support your future stepchildren

✦ Let your fiancé tell his children privately.

✦ Understand if they don't immediately accept you.

✦ Say nice things about their mother.

✦ Don't pressure them to act like a family.

❧ KIDS TALK ❧

My dad told me about his engagement over E-mail. I understand why he did it—I was away at school, and he wanted me to know right away. But still, I wish he would have told me in person. It's a pretty big moment. I would have liked to have felt a part of it.

—*Scott, 19*

An Age-by-Age Guide to
What Your Children Feel and
Need When You Remarry

The kind of support your children need from you regarding your engagement and remarriage will vary according to their ages and developmental stages. The following developmental stages of children and young adults are grouped roughly according to age. Child development experts stress that, especially in adolescence, the exact chronological years of each stage can vary. Your children may fit more into a group slightly above or below their chronological ages. Although death and divorce are different types of losses, many aspects of grieving apply to both situations—take what is useful for your children in your particular circumstance.

INFANCY TO 2 YEARS

How children this age feel and act: A child this age isn't very verbal, but can readily pick up on your emotions and the tension in her environment. She may react by clinging, crying more, or regressing in developmental abilities, like toilet training. At this age, a child is learning trust and feels anxious around strangers. Remember that "Terrible Twos" love to say "no!" It's their first sense of themselves as separate persons who are able to reject and choose.

Helpful responses from you: Don't expect a 1- or 2-year-old to go to your fiancé willingly. The fuss she puts up just means she trusts you and hasn't learned to trust him yet. Accept her need to cling and give her extra cuddles and time with you. If your 2-year-old tells your fiancé, "No! I don't like you!" don't take it personally. She probably says that about cookies, too. Bringing her into new environments, like your fiancé's house, may be additionally upsetting. Keep her in a stable, familiar environment, and she'll feel more outgoing.

AGES 2 TO 6

How children this age feel and act: A child this age can't distinguish between what is real and what is fantasy. He engages in "magical thinking"—he feels responsible for whatever happens. If he wants your fiancé out of the house, he may yell and scream and throw a tantrum about it. It isn't misbehaving; to him, if he wants it strongly, it should happen. He also doesn't have well-developed long-term memory and may need repetition and patient explanations.

Helpful responses from you: A child this age is not a diplomat. He'll say, "Bob has bad breath, I don't like him," and "I liked Daddy better." Don't react with shrieks and tell him those aren't nice things to say. Try, "We're getting used to Bob. We liked some things about Daddy better. What do we like about Bob?" Let your child know that he can still love Daddy, miss Daddy, and see Daddy (if you're divorced). Your fiancé is an extra, new friend—not a new daddy.

AGES 6 TO 9

How children this age feel and act: At about age 7, a child can be logical with some consistency. You can reason with her, as long as you keep it simple. A 7-year-old has begun to realize that others feel differently than she does. Death, divorce, and remarriage are real, as is fear of separation from you: You, too, could die or abandon her to go off with your fiancé.

Helpful responses from you: Though your first husband's death or your divorce may be years behind you, now is when your child may begin to show grief that seems grown-up—

tears, sadness, regret. Sit with her when she's sad and talk about your own sad feelings. If she feels that you understand how she misses Dad on weekends, she may feel more comfortable moving on to accept your fiancé. Comfort her separation anxiety by devoting extra time to her.

AGES 9 TO 12

How children this age feel and act: When a child this age sustains a loss or feels anxious about a major change, fear and separation anxieties often occur. He may seem more clumsy and uncoordinated than usual, take to daydreaming, even have trouble at school. He'll want desperately to fix what feels bad, but won't know how to do it.

Helpful responses from you: Let him know that his feelings and reactions are natural and that change can be upsetting. Tell him, "This feeling is really big and scary, but you need to know that it won't always be this strong. When it is strong, come find me and get a hug." Snuggling, hugs, and closeness are important to all children, but may be especially welcome at this age.

YOUNG TEENS: 12 TO 15

How children this age feel and act: The emotional forces at work in early adolescence are powerful: As they yell at you about how they hate everything you stand for, they simultaneously long for your love and support. They may engage in risky behavior, like staying out late or trying alcohol and drugs. They may feel protective of a parent, especially an opposite-sex parent, and view stepparents as interlopers. As a teen's own sexuality is emerging, the thought of Mom or Dad being romantically involved can seem pretty gross.

Helpful responses from you: Think of reacting to a teen as a test of how mature and adult *you* can be. You are modeling adult behavior for a teen who is acutely interested in how adults react to life. Try not to descend into immature behavior, like yelling and throwing tantrums of your own. Be truthful, direct, and respectful of both your teen and yourself. "I want to know how you feel, but it's hard for me to listen when you scream. Bring it down a few notches, and you've got my complete attention." "You think I've forgotten all about Dad, and that makes you angry with me. Dad will always be important to me, and I'll always love him. But I feel like it's time for me to try to be with someone again." Teens also want hugs and physical closeness, but they have an increased need for privacy and personal space, so ask first.

MIDDLE TEENS: 15 TO 17

How children this age feel and act: Family activities and the desires of parents take a backseat to what his peer group has planned. Anything that makes him feel different in front of his friends—being the kid with one parent or being the kid whose "elderly" mother is getting remarried—is taboo, and it's your fault it happened.

Helpful responses from you: If you plan a big Meet-My-New-Fiancé-Bob activity for the same afternoon your teen has planned an outing with friends, expect fireworks. Instead, invite him to compare calendars in a grown-up way. "I'd like to find a time when you and I can get together with Bob, and I want you to commit to being there. So, you tell me the day that works best for you." Appreciate what's hard for him, and help him see that the two of you will get through it. "It feels really odd to have me dating at the same time you are, doesn't it?" Encourage him to notice that at least half the other kids at school have stepparents, too.

OLDER TEENS: 17 TO 20

How children this age feel and act: Teens this age move away from home, off to college or a job, which creates powerful separation issues and fears. Mom's engagement can feel like the last straw. Many teens this age are sexually active and increasingly aware of the sexual component of Mom's new relationship. Just as your teen becomes aware of her own sexual desires, she faces tangible evidence that you have them, too—which can embarrass her.

Helpful responses from you: Encourage her to live her own life, but let her know she'll always have a place in your home, regardless of who you marry. Keep your parent-child boundaries and don't confess your sexual secrets to her. And even if she is a young woman, and even if he is six feet tall, teens still need hugs and kisses from their parents. Deliver a few.

YOUNG ADULTS: 20 TO 30

How children this age feel and act: Though a 20-year-old looks grown, many are still moving through stages of adolescence. The desire to be independent, coupled with the fear of failing, can still create erratic, teenage-style behavior. A 20-something is involved in his own life, but sees you as his roots. If you are busy rerooting yourself with a new spouse, he may feel unsettled.

Helpful responses from you: In praising your fiancé, don't trash your ex or diminish your child's memories of a deceased parent. Respect your child's memories of his family; he still needs those roots to grow. "Your Dad would be so proud to see you graduate from college. I'm sorry he can't be here. If I bring Sam to the ceremony, will that feel like an intrusion on family time to you?"

GROWN ADULTS: 30 AND BEYOND

How adult children feel and act: Adult children in their 30s and 40s can have surprisingly strong reactions to changes in their parents' love relationships. Your child may wish you would find happiness again after her dad died, but may feel disloyal about liking your fiancé and resentful of having to make room in the family for a new person.

Helpful responses from you: If you make changes to the family home—your fiancé hangs new wallpaper, for example—be aware that you are tinkering with memories, and that doing so may spark some grief and anger. You'll still get to lead your own life, of course, but be patient with short-lived, childlike reactions from your children. Respect your child's memories of the family. Demonstrate that your life can go on without wiping out your shared history with your child.

❧ KIDS TALK ❧

This is embarrassing to admit, but one of my first thoughts when Dad told us he was remarrying was, "Will your new wife get all Mom's things?" I started to think about Mom's heirloom china and her mother's crystal, and I didn't want to think of those things going to someone who wasn't *really* in our family. I felt like a selfish person thinking that, but think it I did, to the point of tears. When Dad told me that he would store Mother's things for my sisters and myself, I immediately relaxed.

—Kris, 48

Telling Your Parents

You announce your engagement to your family and let your fiancé tell his. If your parents are going to flinch, groan, throw up, throw a tantrum, or begin a lengthy diatribe about how they were really fond of your first husband and why the heck did you ever get rid of him, anyway, why subject the new hubby-to-be to all that? And if *his* mother is going to have a fit about you, you'd probably rather not be there, either.

Each of you tell your family separately. Then throw a party or drop by as a couple and make the announcement in a more official and fun manner.

If your parents do object (no, you don't outgrow this—my mother grumbled when it was my fourth engagement and I was 40!), listen to your parents' concerns respectfully and answer their questions if you can. If your parents adored your ex and never understood why you divorced the guy, ask them to understand that, for you, the past is the past and you'd like their support for your new and exciting future.

But if they can't be supportive of you two, tell them that you love them, but you are still going to make the choices that you feel are right for you. Try not to burn any bridges if you can. If it can't be avoided, let your parents know that your door is open, whenever they can make their peace with your new life.

My husband's mother, bless her heart, once took me on a tour of her house, showing me every little gift and knick-knack that my husband's ex had ever bought her. She went on and on about how wonderful my husband's former wife was, despite my husband's frantic signals to her behind my back. My mother-in-law really didn't mean to offend me, she was just sharing happy memories.

Blended families can stymie grandparents

The idea of complicated stepfamilies may confuse your parents. They may not be sure how to act toward your ex when they see him at your son's ball game or toward their new step-grandchildren. Be patient with them and explain to both your fiancé and your future stepchildren that your folks love them, even if they do make the occasional faux pas. Agree as a family that you're going to give the grandparents some slack.

Let your parents know that you intend to treat your future stepchildren as if they are your own and ask your parents to act as though they were lucky enough to be gifted with some additional, instant grandchildren. If your parents choose to give your children holiday gifts but not give gifts to your stepchildren or include your children in social plans but leave your stepchildren out, the result may be serious rifts and terribly hurt feelings. Explain this situation to your parents and ask your fiancé to explain it to his.

If your parents do act out, or just act clueless, take your children and stepchildren aside at once and let them know that to *you*, you're all one big family. You aren't taking the place of your stepchildren's mother, and your fiancé won't take the place of your children's father, but together, you do create your own family unit and others should recognize and honor it. When they don't, you all band together to support each other. Don't support the person hurting you—support each other.

If your parents hated your ex

Your parents may feel this is a terrific moment to rehash every fault your ex had. Try to discourage them from doing so and don't allow it to happen in front of your children. Instead, ask your parents to join in conversations about wedding plans and your happy future.

Telling Your Friends

Once all family members know your good news, call or write your friends with your big announcement. It will be fun to share the good news!

You may have a friend or two who receives your news with less enthusiasm. She or he may have seen you through your divorce or your grief and is hoping you'll avoid any additional pain in the future. Once all your friends have a chance to meet your fiancé and get to know him, he'll likely win them over.

❧ Don't ❧

- Don't announce your engagement before your divorce is final.

- Don't wear an engagement ring before your divorce (or his) is final.

- Don't forget to let your ex (and his) know your plans. If they learn your news from the children, sparks may fly!

- Don't tell your ex the news while the children are in the room.

We met in our 40s. We each already had children. Mine were pretty much grown, and Margaret's were in high school. I just figured they were old enough that they'd deal with our marriage like it was no big deal. *Big* miscalculation! Her girls had seemed so sweet to me while we were dating. But once I got under their roof, it was a war zone. I had certain beliefs about how they should treat their mother, what their curfew should be, and so on, and I tried to enforce those beliefs. Margaret, I think, thought I was being a little tough on the girls. I felt pretty unappreciated. Then, the girls' father decided the girls should live with us full time. Frankly, I had liked my time alone with Margaret. It's pretty hard to be newlyweds with children. The kids expect you to have a working family system down, and you're still trying to create it. The little bumps and rough spots that newlyweds work out together, we had to work out in front of the kids.

—*Stan, 49*

❖ Don't run off to Las Vegas to elope and cut the children out of your wedding.

❖ Don't move your fiancé into your house before the children have even met him.

❧ ETIQUETTE NOTES ❧

If your previous husband died, you may remake your old wedding and engagement rings into new jewelry settings or save them for your children, but don't continue to wear them as rings.

Even if things are going well, consider a preemptive visit with a therapist who specializes in blended families. Two or three sessions now can give you and your fiancé enough information and skills to carry you through years.

CHAPTER FOUR

LET THE PLANS BEGIN!

Determining Your Wedding Style, Finances, Wedding Coordinator, Guest Lists, and Wedding Party Members

Determining Your Wedding Style

The variety of wedding, reception, and honeymoon decisions ahead of you may seem bewildering. Before you become immersed in specifics (and get a major headache), stop and imagine the big picture. Plan a pleasant lunch or afternoon walk with your fiancé during which you can together envision the wedding of your dreams. What suits your personal style? What kind of parties do you enjoy? What are your priorities for the day? How can you design your day so you enjoy yourselves and relax? How can you design your day so your children enjoy themselves and are at their best?

Use your experience to make it a great party

One of the real pluses about no longer being a 22-year-old first-time bride is that you now have some experience throwing terrific parties. Not only did you oversee your own first wedding, but you've been to quite a few other weddings and seen what you liked and didn't like. You've likely also been to corporate gatherings, special events, charity functions, anniversary parties, and graduation open houses—all the while learning what works and what doesn't when you're trying to host and entertain a crowd.

Another terrific thing about being at least a *little* older than you were when you first married is that you have polished and refined your own personal sense of style. Whereas a 22-year-old bride's wedding may reflect her mother's taste, yours will reflect your own and the style of living that you and your fiancé embrace.

Many wedding planners and bridal shop consultants admit a special fondness for working with second-time brides. "She knows what she wants, she's secure about her own taste, and she and her fiancé already have interesting lives," says one. "Those are all the elements of a great party! It's easier and more fun to plan menus, decor, dresses, and the ceremony when you're both grown-ups with established personalities on your own."

This time, it's your wedding

Your colors were pink and chartreuse, your maid of honor was a second cousin you never liked, and your reception menu was *bor-ing!* If you yielded the power of decision making at your first wedding to your mother, mother-in-law, or best friend, here's your chance to do it all over again—your way.

Consider your budget. Some sites and services cost less at different times of the day. For example, serving a wedding breakfast is a less expensive proposition than serving a three-course sit-down dinner. Some wedding and reception sites may be more available in the mornings than in the evenings, or may offer off-season rates.

Consider your wedding style. If you love the idea of a candlelit, formal ceremony and an elegant dinner, a 10 A.M. wedding is not for you.

Consider your children. Choose a time of day for your wedding and reception when they are typically rested, happy, and active (or engage a sitter to take them home from the reception when it's bedtime).

Once you settle on a way that you both want your wedding to *feel* as an event, your decisions about food, flowers, dress, and decoration will follow.

Do you have any strong feelings about anything that happened at your last wedding that you do or do not want to occur this time?	
What budget range are you comfortable with?	

Who Pays for What?

Traditional finances for a first wedding

The bride and/or brid, family covers:

✤ Bride's dress, headdress, accessories

✤ All reception costs

✤ Flowers for the bridesmaids, ceremony site, and reception site

✤ Musicians

✤ Groom's ring and wedding gift

✤ Bridesmaids' gifts

✤ Photographs

✤ Invitations

✤ Ceremony and reception transportation and parking

Right after we announced our engagement, I suddenly felt overwhelmed by all the details of planning a wedding. My mother started asking me questions, like where we were going to hold the wedding and what we would serve at the reception, and I just didn't know how my fiancé Karl and I were going to get all those details decided. Then Karl and I went to dinner by ourselves one night and just started to daydream about what our "ideal" wedding day would be like. We discovered that we each had roughly the same concept: a long weekend with lots of friends, not too much pomp and circumstance, good food, a relaxed atmosphere. It was like we found the "theme" of our wedding. After that conversation, all our other decisions, big and small, sort of fell into place.

—*Deb, 41*

The groom and/or groom's family covers:

+ Marriage license

+ Bride's rings and wedding gift

+ Ushers' gifts (if a formal wedding, also ties and gloves)

+ Flowers for the bride, mothers and grandmothers, and ushers

+ Celebrant's fee

+ Rehearsal dinner

+ Honeymoon

Finances for a second (or subsequent) wedding

There are no hard-and-fast rules. Often, remarrying couples pay for their wedding themselves, sharing the expenses between the two of them. Your parents are not obligated to pay for your second wedding, but may offer to contribute. Your fiancé's parents are not obligated to cover the same expenses they would at a first wedding, but may also offer to help out.

❧ Etiquette Note ❧

If this is your first wedding and your fiancé's second, your parents may finance the ceremony and reception, if they wish.

How do you budget for a wedding?

There are so many elements of a wedding—clothing, travel, catering, photography, music, and more—that it is difficult to arrive at a clear dollar figure in a short time. Weddings are like big parties—they can cost tens of thousands of dollars, a few thousand dollars, or a few hundred dollars. Call several florists, caterers, reception sites, musicians, and photographers to get a range of prices. Pin down specific numbers when you interview and select vendors.

Don't assume that your fiancé is thinking about your wedding budget in the same way you are. Talk together about projected costs and come up with a range with which you are both comfortable.

Do agree with your fiancé on a budget *before* you fall in love with ceremony and reception plans.

Saving money

Once you've completed your **Wedding Day Options Work-sheet** and have a sense of your priorities and those of your fiancé, let these priorities guide you in what to include and what to cut out of your wedding plans. Here are some ways you may save money:

- ❖ Limit the number of guests.

- ❖ Plan an afternoon wedding at which you serve only tea, punch, cake, and canapés.

- ❖ Ask each vendor: "Can you suggest how we may get this kind of result for less money?" or "Are there any ways we can reduce costs?"

- ❖ Choose a nonpopular day of the week or time of the year (reception sites and other vendors may offer reduced fees for weddings on Sundays or "slow" times of the year).

- ❖ Choose flowers that are in season.

- ❖ Limit your professional photographer to one or two hours and augment your album with candid shots taken by your friends and family.

- ❖ Don't serve liquor at your reception or serve only wine and champagne.

- Serve champagne for your toast only; then switch to wine.

- A home reception *may* save you money, but may cost so much in home improvements, rentals, extra help, and stress that you would have been better off in a hotel ballroom.

- Half your wedding costs are likely to be tied to your reception; make cost-effective reception decisions, and your costs will drop.

As you search for ways to save dollars, keep things in perspective. You won't be getting married *that* often and probably never to this guy again. (I can say things like that; I've been married four times.) Your wedding day should be a day of wonderful memories. If you cut too many corners, you're going to remember inconvenience and imperfection. Be reasonable, but also let yourselves create a beautiful day that you'll both enjoy.

Should You Hire a Wedding Coordinator?

If you love throwing a great party, you're probably looking forward with delight to planning every detail of your wedding. But if you already feel overworked and overwhelmed, consider using the services of a good wedding coordinator. Some coordinators like to manage the entire wedding, from announcing the engagement through making the honeymoon reservations. A coordinator can often take your date and run with it, arranging a caterer, photographer, florist, and every-

Mike and I didn't have a huge wedding budget, since we were paying for it ourselves. My folks gave us our wedding cake, my sisters were the musicians, and a friend "catered" our reception by showing up with friends who served and cleaned up. Mike's parents gave us a weekend away at a romantic bed-and-breakfast as our honeymoon, which was a lovely gesture. Our wedding was relaxed and family centered, just like we wanted.

—*Paula, 33*

thing else. Other coordinators are willing to handle only the portions of the planning you want to relinquish. Ask friends for recommendations or open the yellow pages; then interview the coordinator and see if you'd like to work together.

Remember that many wedding ceremony sites and most hotels and reception sites have coordinators whose job is to help you make decisions and remember every detail. Some caterers also enjoy arranging for decorations, floral arrangements, linens, and other details. Bridal shop sales associates can help coordinate your dress with your mother's, your future mother-in-law's, your bridesmaids', and your children's. They can also offer advice about what the men should wear and direct your groom to suitable formal-wear shops. This kind of help often does not cost extra and may be as much support as you need.

Also, remember that you're not 21 any more. This is a good thing. A young bride doesn't have the experience planning social events that you've probably had by now. You may be surprised by how much you'll enjoy the planning during the months ahead.

Oh, and your family and friends will scold me if I forget to mention this: Ask for help! Everybody gets a little misty-eyed about a wedding. Share the romantic glow! Delegate an errand here and there when you've got lots to do. Let family and friends join in the fun. And don't assume that your mother doesn't want to help with wedding number 2—she may just be waiting until you ask.

Who can help?

In a second (or more) wedding, you can use all the help you can get! The duties of your maid of honor, best man, and other family members can expand to include helping with your plans and your children. Be creative! Friends and family often love to be included in wedding arrangements, so let them assist you by baby-sitting while you dress shop, helping track down addresses for guests, running errands, and the like. And don't overlook your groom—second weddings are often planned and executed more by couples than by just the bride. Could your fiancé take your son to the tuxedo shop to be measured and fitted and turn it into a bonding outing with a ball game afterward?

The secret to turning the coming months into a bonding, growing time for your blended family-to-be is to delegate, delegate, delegate. Get your children, your fiancé, your family, and your friends involved. Everyone loves a wedding!

❧ KIDS TALK ❧

My mom and I went shopping for my junior bridesmaid dress. We spent two nights making little bags of birdseed for people to toss at the wedding. We went to a spa together before the wedding to get our nails and facials done. We had a lot of fun together before her wedding!

—*Kara, 16*

The Guest List: What, *Another* Wedding of Yours?

My friends like to complain at parties that, considering how often I throw a wedding reception for myself, they have never been to my nuptials. No, I didn't invite all the same people to all four of my weddings. Friends can fly cross-country only so many times.

How many guests?

The number of guests you invite will affect your budget like no other number. If you want a crowd, then invite them, but realize that you may have to consider an afternoon tea reception, rather than a sit-down dinner, if your budget is constrained. You may certainly invite as many guests as you wish and as your pocketbook allows, but a second or subsequent wedding gives you an opportunity to scale down without offending anyone. People expect that a second wedding will be a smaller affair than your first. If you can scale your guest list down far enough, here's your chance to throw a totally elegant party for twenty-five or fifty guests. But if you can't cut back that far, no one will judge you. Go ahead and invite the number of guests you desire.

Keeping track of gifts

You may prefer to add two more columns to your list: space for writing in shower gifts and wedding gifts. Check off when you've sent a thank-you note for each.

Guests' Names	Number of Guests	Number of Invitations Needed	Shower Gifts	Wedding Gifts
Bob and Mary Carlton and children: Tom, 12, and Shelly, 7	3 adults, 1 child	1 Bob, Mary, Shelly 1 Tom	Linen table-cloth √ thank-you note sent	2 crystal flutes √ thank-you note sent

❧ ETIQUETTE NOTE ❧

Anyone who is invited to your bridal shower should also be invited to your wedding.

Who's invited?

Start with you, your fiancé, your children, and your families. If your wedding is to be small, you can limit invitations to immediate family members and omit extended family members. You decide where to draw the line.

Once you've listed family members, start adding friends. If anyone seems "iffy," make a mark next to his or her name on your list. If the list gets too long, you can omit that person.

If your wedding is to be large, you can offer your parents and your fiancé's parents the opportunity to invite guests.

However, for an encore wedding, this is optional. That social "debt" was probably paid by your first wedding.

❧ ETIQUETTE NOTE ❧

Yes, you should invite your celebrant to the reception. However, unless he or she is a close friend of your family or your groom's family, your celebrant is unlikely to attend. Hand deliver an addressed invitation to the celebrant and spouse yourself.

Everyone else's children

If you and your fiancé have young children who'll be present at your ceremony and reception, you'll be making special arrangements for them: a baby-sitter to attend to them, a special menu and table at the reception, and so forth. These arrangements can be extended to include any other children you invite, if you wish.

Just because your children will be present doesn't mean you have to invite the children of every guest. You can invite your own nieces, nephews, and grandchildren, yet not invite those of your guests—it's proper. You can invite certain children you especially adore and not invite others. It's like any guest list—invite who you want.

Divorced parents and other tricky problems

If you or your fiancé have parents who are separated, divorced, widowed, or remarried, you may wonder how to handle wedding situations. The best solution would be if everyone agreed to act civilized and get along so that you and your fiancé could enjoy your wedding. Your family and guests ought to be focused on you and your happy day, not on their usual social preferences. Hey, you can always hope.

There are etiquette rules to guide you through some of the sticky wickets, but if the rules themselves create problems, toss 'em out in favor of family harmony. In each chapter, suggestions for how to handle various situations (invitations, seating, who walks you down the aisle, and the like) include what to do if your parents are not Ward and June Cleaver.

You're going to run into some people who aren't comfortable socializing with some of your other guests. If your parents are divorced, your mother probably doesn't typically lunch with your dad's new wife. If you are still pretty friendly with your ex-in-laws, you probably don't often entertain them at the same time as you do your parents. In these types of situations, making seating arrangements at tables ahead of time and putting name cards at the place settings can head off a certain amount of awkwardness.

If you suspect that your parents or family may be made uncomfortable at the ceremony or reception, talk with them ahead of time. You may find the air clearer than you think. As a young teen, my daughter confessed to me that she was worried (well in advance) about her wedding. "You and Dad will never both show up in the same place!" she complained. Since her father and I have long been mutually present at her school concerts, plays, and sporting events, why she thought we wouldn't both show up at her wedding, I don't know. Though her highly premature worry seemed a little silly at the time, it gave me a chance to reassure her that her Dad and I would *always* be present whenever she wanted us to be, regardless of how we were feeling about each other that week.

If anyone dares to threaten you with that "I won't come if you invite *her*" third-grade level of social behavior, try to calm the storm with straight talk. "This is my wedding, not your battleground. I care about each of you and want you both to be there. I'd consider it a big 'I love you' message if you'd please attend."

Inviting your ex or your fiancé's ex, no matter how Sonny-and-Cher you all are about it, is just not a great idea. It's likely to make your children feel at least a little schizophrenic, for one thing. And it will probably detract focus and attention from you and your new union as your guests watch your ex's every move and wait for fireworks.

If your former spouse or your fiancé's former spouse died and you are still close with your former in-laws, you can certainly invite them.

❧ TIP ❧

If you've got a particularly sticky situation with divorced parents who don't want to appear together at your wedding, share with them how you plan to separate them in seating arrangements during your ceremony and reception. Once they realize that they won't have to share the same pew or table, they may relax and tensions may ease.

Your Wedding Party

At your first wedding, you may have felt obligated to invite certain family members and friends to be part of your wedding party. At your second wedding, such real or imagined obligations no longer exist. Do what you like!

You may have a large wedding party or just designate one person as your attendant/witness. You may involve your children or ask your best friend. A woman I know who has only one sibling, a brother, asked him to be her "maid of honor." The only hard-and-fast rules are those you make for yourself.

Married or even visibly pregnant attendants are appropriate. Just select a dress that will be the correct size for your pregnant attendant at the time of your wedding.

How many members do you need in your wedding party?

You'll want enough ushers to seat guests without making other guests wait—about one usher for every twenty to twenty-five guests. You may have as many or as few bridesmaids as you wish. A large wedding party signals a formal wedding and a large guest list. A small wedding may have only a maid of honor and a best man. You may even have no one in your wedding party and ask family members or good friends to sign your license with you as witnesses.

You don't need even numbers

You need not have exactly as many bridesmaids as ushers. If your numbers are not even, just work out your processional and recessional so that no one feels awkward. One bridesmaid can be escorted by two ushers, or your ushers can exit separately from your bridesmaids.

If one of your bridesmaids or groomsmen drops out of your wedding party suddenly, asking someone else to be an overnight replacement can make them feel like a "B" list friend. It's fine to go ahead with the ceremony without one wedding party member. You don't need an even number of bridesmaids and ushers.

What Your Wedding Party Can Do for You

There are traditional roles associated with each member of a wedding party. If these roles aren't quite right for you, let each member of the wedding party know how you'd like him or her to be involved.

Duties of wedding party members

MAID OR MATRON OF HONOR

1. If you aren't a family member, you may choose to give the bride a bridal shower or a party before the wedding.

2. Consider yourself a "girl Friday," helping the bride with anything and everything from choosing a dress months before the wedding to pressing her hankie the morning of the ceremony. Ask the bride what you can do to help before, during, and after the wedding.

3. Learn what the bride wants you to wear; then make a selection accordingly. If you and the bridesmaids are wearing matching outfits, be measured for yours on time. Payment for your outfit is your responsibility.

4. If you and the bridesmaids wish to give the bride a

gift from all of you, organize collecting money, choosing a gift, and giving it to the bride (probably at a bridesmaids' luncheon or party).

5. If there is a rehearsal, be there. If there is a rehearsal dinner, attend.

6. Help the bride dress on the wedding day. Pack an emergency kit of pantyhose, nail polish, sewing kit, lipstick, aspirin, hair spray, and whatever else you think she may need. You'll be a lifesaver!

7. Make sure the bride eats something before the ceremony. Keep her drinking water, too—though not immediately before the ceremony!

8. Keep the groom's wedding ring for safekeeping.

9. Help the bride arrange her dress and flowers before her entrance.

10. Hold the bride's bouquet during the ceremony.

11. Stand in the receiving line and greet guests. Introduce each guest to the bridesmaid on your right.

12. Pose cheerfully in pictures.

13. Help the bride change from her wedding dress to her going-away outfit. Take time to hang her wedding dress carefully and collect all the little bits and pieces of clothing, makeup, and so on. Return the dress to her home while she is on her honeymoon.

BRIDESMAIDS

1. If you aren't a family member, you may choose to give the bride a bridal shower or a party before the wedding.

2. Learn what the bride wants you to wear; then make a selection accordingly and/or be measured for yours on time. Payment is your responsibility.

3. Ask the bride what you can do to help before, during, and after the wedding.

4. If there is a rehearsal, be there. If there is a rehearsal dinner, attend.
5. Stand in the receiving line and greet guests. Introduce each guest to the bridesmaid on your right.
6. Pose cheerfully in pictures.

BEST MAN

1. Arrange for your own clothing and help communicate clothing requirements to the groomsmen and ushers.
2. If you wish, throw a party for the groom early in the week before the wedding (the night before is a bad, bad idea).
3. If there is a wedding rehearsal, attend it. If there is a rehearsal dinner, attend it.
4. Show up early on the day of the wedding and help the groom with last-minute details. Does he have studs? Cufflinks? The right tie? Socks? Do you? Do the other groomsmen?
5. Help the groom bring his going-away clothes to the reception.
6. Drive the groom to the ceremony.
7. Double-check with the groom to be sure the marriage license is brought to the wedding.
8. Carry the wedding ring and give it to the groom during the ceremony. If there is a ring bearer, carry the ring until just before the ceremony; then tie it onto the ring bearer's pillow and give the pillow to an adult for safekeeping until the moment the ring bearer enters the church.
9. Pose cheerfully in pictures.
10. Get payment for the celebrant from the groom and deliver it. Help the groom by also delivering payment envelopes to the caterer, musicians, and reception site.

11. After the wedding, keep the signed marriage certificate and return it to the groom after the honeymoon.

12. The first toast is yours to make. Don't mention anyone's ex-spouse or first wedding. Say complimentary things to both the bride and groom and wish them love and happiness.

13. If there are any congratulatory letters or telegrams from absent guests, read them aloud at the reception (after your toast would be a good time).

14. Dance with the bride, the mothers, the bridesmaids. Serve as a sort of unofficial host.

15. Drive the bride and groom from the reception to the hotel or airport. Hide the car to prevent excessive "decorating" and be sure it's filled with gas. Sneak a box lunch of food from the caterer into the backseat so the couple can eat on the way.

16. Collect and return your rented formalwear and that of the groom after the wedding. Remind the other ushers to return theirs.

USHERS OR GROOMSMEN

1. Find out from the best man or groom what you are to wear. Arrange for it (be measured, order the tuxedo, and so forth) in a timely manner. Payment is your responsibility.

2. If there is a wedding rehearsal, attend it. If there is a rehearsal dinner, attend it.

3. Show up early on the day of the wedding. Ahead of time, have your studs, cufflinks, socks, shoes, and whatever else you need packed and ready to go.

4. Pose cheerfully in pictures.

5. Await guests at the rear of the church or ceremony site. Offer your right arm to the woman; if she is part

of a couple, the man follows behind. Ask "friend of the bride or groom?" Seat the bride's friends on your left, as you face the altar. Seat the groom's friends on your right. Ask the groom and bride if there are any special seating instructions. Guests who have "reserved pew" cards are seated matching the number on the card to the number on the pew.

6. Once the mother of the bride is seated, if a white runner is to be laid on the center aisle, assist with laying it out. Runners usually come rolled up, with a handle that easily allows you to unroll it. If the runner is laid out before the ceremony, escort guests up the side aisles.

7. Ask the bride and groom if there are special guests, such as grandparents, you should be escorting out of the church or temple after the wedding.

8. Help transport the bridesmaids—and any family members who need rides—to the reception.

RING BEARER

1. Wears a miniature tuxedo or a dress-up suit. His parents pay for his clothes.

2. Carries a pillow with the wedding rings tied onto it. Sometimes, substitute rings are used.

3. Poses cheerfully (you hope!) for pictures

4. If the rehearsal dinner isn't too late, attends it with his parents. Otherwise, his parents may attend "for him."

FLOWER GIRL

1. Wears a dress that is similar to the bridesmaids' but modified for her age or a dress just for her. Her parents pay for her clothes.

2. Carries a basket of real or paper flower petals to scatter on the aisle as she walks

3. Poses cheerfully (you hope!) for pictures
4. If the rehearsal dinner isn't too late, attends it with her parents. Otherwise, her parents may attend "for her."

❧ DON'T ❧

❖ Don't assume there are rigid rules for what you "have" to do at your wedding. One of the delights of a second wedding is that family members and other guests expect that the rules will be bent a little.

❖ Don't forget your mother. Sure, this isn't your first wedding, but she'd probably still like to help and is just waiting for an invitation from you.

❧ RESOURCES ❧

❖ As you and your fiancé begin to explore your wedding style, ask friends and family members for stories about second weddings they've attended. You may get an inspiration!

❖ To find a registered bridal consultant in your area, contact:

Association of Bridal Consultants
200 Chestnutland Road
New Milford, CT 06776
phone (203)355-0464

❖ There's a bridal magazine especially for encore brides. Try the internet and your newsstand for *Bride Again* magazine.

CHAPTER FIVE

I GAVE AT THE FIRST WEDDING

Gifts, Showers, Registries, and Rings

❧

Do shower and wedding gifts matter the second time around?

Yes, to your family and friends, who want to express their love and support for you, for your new family, and for your new love.

You may feel that you don't want people to fuss over you again (after all, they gave at your first wedding). But then again . . . couldn't you use a new blender?

Can You Have a Shower?

Yes, showers and parties are permissible, even for second-time brides!

Though certainly appropriate, showers aren't often given for second-time brides-to-be because your friends and family probably attended a shower for your first wedding and gave you gifts. Also, you are no longer a first-time bride leaving home with little or no belongings of her own—now you have an established household. However, if you live in another town from the one where you first married, have a different circle of friends, or work somewhere you didn't during your first marriage, a shower with new

friends would not seem like asking twice for shower gifts. If a good friend wants to host a shower for you, don't dampen her excitement—go ahead and enjoy!

❧ TIP ❧

Remember to assign a friend the task of recording who gave which gift, so you can write thank-you notes accurately. And send your hostesses a thank-you gift.

Who is invited?

Your hostess will ask you for a list of guests to invite. Include your bridesmaids, all members of your wedding party, your sisters and mother, your stepmother (if you have one and if she and your mother get along), your mother-in-law, and other good friends. If you are given more than one shower, don't invite the same people to both. This situation will likely suggest its own solution. For example, if a bridesmaid is giving the shower, certainly invite all the other bridesmaids. If your college roommate is giving the shower, invite old girlfriends. If your hostess wants your wedding party, sisters, and mother present, even if they have been at another shower for you, let your wedding party and family know that you'll welcome their company but that you don't expect another gift.

❧ ETIQUETTE NOTES ❧

- Any guest you invite to a shower must also receive an invitation to your wedding and reception.

- Showers should be given by friends, not family members.

- Are parties appropriate? Absolutely. But if your divorce or your fiancé's divorce is not yet final, postpone parties and showers until legal matters are completely settled.

Introduce Your Parents

First wedding tradition suggests that the parents of the bride and groom meet for dinner. This is one tradition you should definitely honor the second time around. Your mother and your fiancé's mother may not have as many matters to work out at your wedding as they might have had at a first wedding, but certainly your parents will want to meet one another well before your wedding.

The Awkwardness of
Family and Friends

If you are the first remarried person in your circle of friends or in your family, you may encounter some social awkwardness. Chances are, they are excited and happy for you, but they may not know what to say or how to say it. Prepare yourself for a little conversational bumpiness now and then and accept the good intentions behind the comments.

❧ Kids Talk ❧

My mom was getting all these presents, which made me feel sort of bad for my dad, who was still living in this bare apartment. But now, my dad remarried, too, and he has a nice house.

—Kara, 8

Go Ahead and Register—
No One Knows What You Got
in the Settlement

One of the lovely aspects of marrying at a more advanced age than 18 is that the friends who celebrate with you have probably known you for a good, long while. They know your personality, they know your likes and dislikes, and they know your living style.

But buying for remarrying folk can be challenging. Your Aunt Harriet may guess that you got all the china and crystal that you wanted at your first wedding and give you a magazine subscription instead. But what if your first husband kept your dishes, and you're actually dying for a place setting or two?

Let everyone know what you want: Register at a bridal registry. In the past, such registries existed only at fine department stores and concentrated on china, crystal, silver, and traditional gifts. Today, discount stores, garden shops, cooking stores, and specialty boutiques all have registries and may be more practical in your particular situation. Let a few friends or family know where you're registered, and they'll let everyone else know.

❦ ETIQUETTE NOTE ❦

When you register, choose items in a variety of prices. That way, every guest will be able to find something to give in his or her price range. Silver place settings and some china and crystal settings are expensive. Indicate on your registry form and let the sales staff know that you consider a single piece of silver or of crystal to be a wonderful gift and that guests need not feel they must give you an entire place setting.

What should you register for?

If you and your fiancé already have all the necessities for your new home, you may feel stymied when friends ask for gift ideas or when you register for gifts. When you were first married, practical gifts like linens and tableware were probably your priority. Now that you've been living on your own for some time, it's likely that you don't need towels or dishes. What could you possibly want?

◈ Though you may already have a set of china, choosing dishes, flatware, and crystal together as a couple is a nice symbol of making a fresh life together. Make a romantic afternoon out of choosing tableware for your new life with your fiancé.

Other ideas for gifts include:

◈ Art objects, small sculptures, prints, decorative objects

◈ Picture frames for photos (all the better if they come with photos of your friend in them!)

◈ Photo albums

◈ Linens with your new monogram

◈ Items for your new home: a door knocker, garden ornaments, bird feeders

◈ Things that you and your fiancé share as common interests: sports equipment, theater tickets, museum memberships

◈ Luxury household items: a pasta maker, a cappuccino machine, exotic kitchen gadgets

◈ TIP ◈

If you or your fiancé have family and friends in another town, consider registering there, too.

Where Do You Live?

As you think about registering for wedding gifts, the question of where you're going to live rears its head. Your house? His house? A new house?

If either of you lived in your home with your former spouse, trying to start a new marriage there is a flawed concept. You'll likely feel the ghost of his first wife in the paint color, the living room carpet, the stories ("Lydia and I picked out that fireplace mantel. . . ."). This kind of living arrangement will make it *much* easier for you two to have that inescapable second marriage fight: "If you liked your first wife so much, then why did you marry *me*?"

If either or both of you have children, you're adding miniature territorial terrorists to the situation. Not only will you be bristling at the intruders, but your children will be, too. "You mean I have to share *my* room? With *her*?"

Fresh digs that are new to all of you at the same time can be a tremendous help to a blended family. You'll all make that house into your home at the same time, so no one will feel like an outsider.

Sometimes, economics dictate that you can't buy a new home before your wedding. If one of you has to move in with the other, be especially gentle with each other's feelings at this time. Remind each other and the children that this currently crowded or inconvenient circumstance won't last forever and that you'll all get to choose the new house together soon.

You may not be able to invest in a new home at all. Or perhaps you'll choose one of your homes and decide to live there together permanently. Try to safeguard against the common pitfalls of this kind of situation. No matter how deeply you love each other, one of you is "trespassing" on the other's turf. It's hard to relinquish personal space and let a stranger—even one you love madly—inside. It's hard to move into a strange space and not feel like an interloper. Add children to that mix ("I liked my old bedroom better!" "I used to have my own bathroom!"), and everybody's blood pressure can go up a few notches.

A month before our wedding, Bill moved into the little house I shared with my three children. We certainly knew he was coming and had moved furniture around and cleaned out closet space accordingly. Still, things were cramped. Though Bill was just one more person, he threw off the balance. Four chairs around the kitchen table were no longer enough. One more person taking a shower in the morning made some of us late getting out the door. My bedroom, once my retreat, was now overflowing with his enormous (who knew?) collection of ties—not to mention his shirts, shoes, suits, and two dozen sweaters he never wore but insisted on keeping in plain view. He turned my laundry room into his photo darkroom, which interfered with the flow of clean underwear. He brought home strange groceries. He was loving and generous, and so were my children. But for a while, we kept bumping into each other, figuratively and emotionally. If you can't start from scratch with your living space, set realistic expectations for yourselves and prepare the children with a few discussions about how things may feel and be different after moving day.

If you'll be moving into one of your homes, chances are your space will be tight. Instead of adding more things, you'll probably be putting some in storage and getting rid of others. Though you may feel that this means you shouldn't register for gifts (more stuff!), it may be a great reason *to* do it. Family and friends who know your living situation will want to give you gifts that will actually be useful to you—so register, and let them know what you really need and want.

If you'll be moving into a new house together, it may be easier for you to make decisions about which possessions stay, which go, and what you'll need that you don't have now. You can register for some of these items as wedding gifts, or you can make an adventure out of choosing them together.

Yours, mine, and ours

You hate his dishes, he hates your toaster, and neither of you have pots and pans that hold up under inspection. These are good things to know before you move in together, but they're hard things to hear. Trust me (I'm almost *sure* that I've done it this *way* more times than you), you'll surprise each other and yourselves by how territorial you can feel about mere housewares.

I once married an architect who prefaced our wedding by wandering around my house putting little yellow stickers on the items he would *allow* me to keep (he thought he was the Arbiter of Taste). Hint: This is *not* a good plan.

Yes, you have to start blending your possessions. But rather than drop a bomb ("Your sofa is the ugliest color I've ever seen. You're not thinking of keeping it after the wedding, are you?"), try a little diplomacy. Start by asking your fiancé how *he* envisions your stuff combining. "What do you see us keeping? How do you imagine us deciding what to keep and what to toss?" He may surprise you by volunteering that *he* always hated that dumpy sofa, too, and sees this move as his chance finally to get rid of the thing.

As you stumble through this particular minefield, don't make rash decisions. If he hates your grandmother's china, box it and store it. A year from now, when life has calmed down, he may like it, and you may be in a large enough house to display it again. If he loves that dumpy sofa, put it in storage until you have a house with a family room where you can hide it.

❧ KIDS TALK ❧

I didn't like having to get rid of some of our stuff. That bothered me. But Tom and his kids had some cool things we didn't have. And my Mom took us each shopping for what we needed for our new rooms at Tom's. I liked that.

—*Keith, 9*

Cleaning house

Before you marry, now is the time to clear away mementos and photos of your first marriage. Don't purge thoughtlessly—you may regret it later. Be intentional and consider carefully what's best to do for your new marriage and your children.

Children should certainly have photographs of their missing parent—whether taken away by death or divorce—in their rooms. If your new stepchildren want photos of their mother next to their beds, don't get your ego in a snit. Don't you want *your* children's stepmother to let your children remember and honor you? Your fiancé should not object to your children remembering their dad this way, either.

Family photo albums need not be banished to storage, but do take a close look at the photos you choose to display on your walls, shelves, and tables. Mix in photos of your new family, including your new stepchildren, and winnow out old photos for now. Reintroduce the old photos after some time has passed, but now your new family needs all the support it can get!

Old love letters and romantic cards should be boxed and stored. Unless these notes are too "adult," you may wish to keep them for your children, especially if your first husband died. Tangible evidence that Dad existed and that Mom and Dad loved each other means a great deal to children, even later in life, when they are grown. Don't toss this stuff, but do put it out of sight for now.

Talk to your fiancé about furniture items "left over" from his and your first marriages. Air any strong feelings that either of you have about recycling these items in your new life together. You may have no qualms about using his dining table that he picked out with Wife Number 1, but you'll probably balk at sleeping in their old bed. This is understandable. Buy a new bed.

❧ WRITE THANK-YOU NOTES ❧

You're too old for me to have to tell you this, but always acknowledge a gift (and even a thoughtful favor) with a graciously worded thank-you note. Preprinted thank-you cards are in bad taste. Write a personal note by hand that compliments the gift you received and thanks the giver for his or her thoughtfulness.

❧ Etiquette Notes ❧

- Though you may think that asking for "no gifts" is thoughtful, many people interpret it as being ungracious. Writing "no gifts, please" on your invitation is not appropriate. If you want to put the word out that you aren't expecting gifts and would prefer none, ask a parent or friend to let others know. But including such a wish written on or in your invitation is a no-no.

- If any gift arrives broken, return it to the store and have it replaced without mentioning it to the person who sent it.

- Either the bride or groom may write a thank-you note, but mention both of you. "Laurie and I love the vase you sent . . ."

- Don't keep telling people "they shouldn't have." Thank them for being supportive and for joining in your excitement and happiness.

Rings

Your fiancé may have already presented you with an engagement ring that he chose himself. If you love it, there's no problem. If you don't, be honest and tell him—you'll be wearing this ring for a long time.

If you want to choose your ring together, but you don't want to know what your fiancé spends on it, ask him to call the jeweler ahead of time. The jeweler can select a range of rings in your fiancé's price range, before you go to the store, and you can choose from them.

◈ WEDDING CUSTOM HISTORY ◈

Legend calls the diamond a stone forged in the flames of love—perhaps that's why it's a traditional engagement stone. Each gemstone has its own legend and qualities, however. Garnet and ruby are thought to enhance sexuality and heal the heart. Yellow and golden stones, like citrine, are believed to enhance warmth, openness, and love. Peridot calms the heart and inspires balance. Rose-colored stones are said to attract love and harmony. Emerald was an ancient healing stone in Cleopatra's time, believed to carry peace, love, and joy. Sapphire is thought to deliver clarity and peace. In ancient Greece, opal was a stone of hope and good fortune. Amethyst is a stone of wisdom and energy.

The second time around, there are no special rules about what your engagement and wedding rings should look like. If you like diamonds, choose diamonds. If you prefer a colored stone, wear one. If you and your fiancé want matching bands, have them. Nothing is inappropriate, as long as you two love what you choose.

- ✦ Crate and Barrel
  www.crateandbarrel.com

- ✦ Pier 1 Imports
  www.pier1.com

- ✦ Home Depot
  www.homedepot.com

- ✦ Bed, Bath & Beyond
  www.bedbathandbeyond.com

- ✦ Williams Sonoma
  www.Williams-Sonoma.com

- ✦ Target
  www.target.com

✦ Check the internet for information on buying diamonds and rings.

✦ Two sources for wedding medallions that you and your children may exchange during your ceremony:

Clergy Services, Inc.
706 West 42nd Street
Kansas City, MO 64111
(800)237-1922
or
Dr. Roger Coleman at rcoleman@tfs.net

✦ Some major national retailers offer books to help brides plan their gift registries. On the internet, search for the name of the department store you'd like to register with—there may even be an online registry! Or call your store's china and crystal department to ask if there is a book to help you. One, called *The Wedding Book*, is produced by stores like Macy's and Burdines and other members of the gift registry alliance. For a free copy, call (800)782-4026.

CHAPTER SIX

YOUR WEDDING SITE, CELEBRANT, AND CEREMONY

Reserve Your Dates

You don't need every detail of your wedding settled immediately, but if you're certain of the date and time you want, start reserving the essentials. If you delay, you may miss out on sites or vendors of your choice.

Set up meetings with each contact person to discuss the

The celebrant	____ Reserved wedding date and time	Meeting date: _____
The wedding site	____ Reserved wedding date and time	Meeting date: _____

details in a few days or weeks, depending on how much time you have before your wedding.

Choosing a Wedding Site

An encore bride can be married anywhere that a first-time bride can be married. What's different now is that you may feel more adventurous about your options. Many women want a big church or temple wedding. If you had one the first time, however, you may wish to try an entirely different type of wedding this time. Sometimes, first-time brides feel bound to honor religious, cultural, and family traditions in their wedding plans. Since family members and friends often expect a certain relaxing of tradition for a second wedding, the door is open for you and your fiancé to plan an original wedding that reflects the two of you and your new family.

You can be married nearly anywhere, provided that you have enough space for your guests and a plucky celebrant who is willing to be adventurous. Your community may have a historic home, park, or public garden that is popular for weddings. Ask your caterer, photographer, and florist candidates where they do weddings—you'll net a list of good possibilities. Among your options:

A church or temple

If you or your fiancé belong to a church or temple, this may be your best choice for a ceremony site. In addition to the spiritual, reverent atmosphere and the feeling of being part of a spiritual community, there are practical pluses: seats, aisles, an altar, rooms for dressing, adequate rest room facilities, and good parking. However, if you're each of different faiths, you may wish not to hold your ceremony in a religious building.

A hotel

Hotels are in the business of hosting weddings and are set up to handle most situations. There will be a catering director or special events coordinator on staff to help you make arrangements. You'll probably not have to rent tables, chairs, china, or crystal—most hotel rates include these items. Your florist, musicians, and photographers may have worked at this site before and be familiar with it and its staff.

As an encore bride, you may feel less eager to escape on your honeymoon and more interested in enjoying the friends and family who have traveled to be at your wedding. If you make your wedding into a weekend-long event, a hotel site has advantages. Guests and family can spend the night in rooms and breakfast together in the morning.

A bed-and-breakfast

A small hotel or bed-and-breakfast in a historic home can be a romantic setting for a wedding—with the added feature of rooms for family and friends to dress and spend the night (or weekend) in. Everyone can meet in the dining room for breakfast the next morning and continue the celebrating. Many B&Bs are in beautifully restored and appointed homes, so they provide gorgeous backdrops for photos. You'll want to find a B&B with a parlor, garden, or porch large enough for your wedding party and guests, which may be difficult to do.

If you have children, the homey atmosphere of a B&B may suit your wedding style more than a formal church or hotel site.

Your home

A home wedding has a lovely, personal feeling. Your children will feel relaxed, and if your children are young, you'll be close to nap and child care supplies. The obvious limitations of a home wedding are space, parking, and adequate rest room facilities. If you have a home with a living room, dining room, or other space large enough for your ceremony, then you're in luck. Check with your celebrant to be sure that he or she is willing to celebrate a wedding in a private home. Check over your home and garden with a critical eye, measuring all the touch-up and maintenance work you would need to do before your wedding day. Are you willing to put yourself and your family through that? If you choose a home wedding, strongly consider bringing in a caterer to manage the event and the refreshments for you.

Outdoors

Being married in a gorgeous outdoor site is a romantic idea. There's a practical side to it, too: Your children can run around, make noise, and not seem disruptive or inappropriate. But hosting a wedding outdoors does present some practical problems. As you make your plans, be sure you've considered all the angles:

1. Can your guests easily find this place? A country meadow is charming, but will everyone get there in time?
2. Is there enough parking? Parks, outdoor gazebos, and flower gardens sometimes have little or no parking, forcing guests in high heels, dresses, and suits to hike for blocks.

3. If the weather is bad, where will you go? If you're thinking of an outdoor site, plan for inclement weather with a tent or an outbuilding. Remember that very hot weather, though not a reason to stop the ceremony, can certainly make everyone uncomfortable.

4. Will you be interrupted by nonguests? Will your arboretum wedding be interrupted by grubby gardeners strolling through? Your beach wedding vows drowned out by the lifeguard's loudspeaker?

5. Will guests be able to hear your vows? Outdoors, your voices may not carry without microphones.

6. Will your celebrant come to this site? If your clergy member won't officiate in a park or public hotel, you may need to consider a judge or other official.

7. Will you be there long enough to need to provide rest room facilities?

8. Where will the wedding party dress?

9. Can you transport flowers there?

10. What kind of music is portable and doesn't require electricity?

If you want to be married in a public space—a lakeshore, park, or garden—call the Parks and Recreation office of your city or county to reserve the space.

If you want to hold your reception outdoors, as well, hire a caterer with experience in serving fancy picnics. Your caterer will need refrigeration equipment for food and drinks, portable glasses, tables, and chairs, among other equipment.

Destination weddings

In bridal magazines, you'll see advertisements for destination weddings: traveling to a glamorous vacation spot for a wedding and honeymoon, all in one. One attractive feature of a destination wedding for a busy two-career couple is that many destinations (such as theme parks and vacation resorts) have staff on hand who handle all the details of planning your wedding and reception for you. However, there *is* a big reason why parents who are marrying would want to bypass a destination ceremony. If you and/or your fiancé have children, they should be present at your wedding, surrounded by your family and friends. Their presence gives your union and your children much needed support. With a destination wedding, your only wedding guests are going to be those who can afford to travel there with you. And you'll be missing a side benefit of planning your own wedding. Those weeks and months of making arrangements allow you, your fiancé, and your combined children to "try on" the idea of becoming a family. Planning and working together can be a fun, bonding experience.

Choosing a Celebrant

If both you and your fiancé attend the same church or temple and both want to be married there, this won't be an issue you need to resolve. If you belong to different churches or temples but don't feel strongly about which site to choose for your wedding, interview both about their wedding customs and rules and check your potential dates with the two. If you are of different faiths, you may want to consider having a celebrant of each faith present at your wedding.

If you or your fiancé are educating your children in a certain faith, marrying in that faith would be a message of consistency to your children. If your fiancé is of a different faith than you and your children, incorporating elements of both faiths into your ceremony sends a message of respect to your children and sets an important tone for your new family.

Such interfaith ceremonies have become common. If a celebrant at your church or temple does not want to participate in such a blended ceremony, ask other celebrants in the area. Within the same faith and even within the same parish or area, clergy set different requirements and have different attitudes toward interfaith marriages.

If your wedding will be at a church, temple, or chapel, you are likely to use a celebrant on staff there. Ask if a particular celebrant enjoys performing second-wedding ceremonies or has a special interest in incorporating children into ceremonies.

If you are a member of a congregation, your church or temple may require that you and your fiancé attend a series of premarital counseling sessions with the celebrant. Some churches waive this requirement with a second wedding. When you reserve your church or temple for your wedding date, inquire about this and any other requirements. Also, record the name and number of the celebrant's secretary or assistant. This is often the person who is assigned to answer questions about the details of the ceremony ("Can my father speak during the wedding?" "Which door receives floral deliveries?").

Your church or temple may even have a packet of informational materials that will answer most of your questions about your ceremony. When you meet with your celebrant, use the worksheet in this chapter to answer all your questions.

Other options for celebrants

Besides a priest, rabbi, minister, pastor, iman, or other church officiant, your wedding (depending on the laws in your area) may be performed by:

- A mayor

- A city clerk

- A court clerk

- A justice or judge

- A marriage officer (a civic position)

❖ Do ❖

Do try to make the best of a disaster. Something is sure to go at least partly wrong, but that's what a great wedding day story is made of. My husband's parents were married just after World War II ended, in a lovely cathedral in Green Bay, Wisconsin. When my mother-in-law arrived at the church that morning, she was horrified to discover that the interior was about to be painted and that an elaborate metal and wood scaffolding had been erected all over the inside of the church. At the time, she was furious that she had been told nothing about it. But an enterprising photographer climbed up into the choir loft to shoot the wedding party through the scaffolding as they entered, taking an extraordinary photograph that would never had existed otherwise. That *is* a great story!

A ceremony program

You may wish to create a program for your ceremony that lists who sings, speaks, and serves in your wedding party. If there are songs or prayers you wish your guests to participate in, this is a good place to print them. Your program may also include a mention of your children.

Your wedding program may be as simple or elaborate as you wish. Some printers of invitations also produce programs and offer designs that coordinate with your invitations. A simple list of events printed in an elegant typeface on a computer printer is also acceptable.

Have your programs passed to guests by your children, set them at the entrance of the ceremony site, or display them in a basket where guests may easily find them.

❧ TIP ❧

If your church or temple does not allow flash photography during wedding ceremonies, you'll have discussed this with your own photographer. But guests may not be aware of this rule. Make special mention of it in your wedding program, if you have one, or have a calligrapher create a tasteful sign that you can post at the entrance.

Wedding Site and Celebrant Interview Worksheet

Which of our potential dates and times work for you? How much flexibility do you have if we find we have to change the date? Are there any date restrictions (no weddings during Lent, no ceremonies on Sunday, and so forth)?	
Do you need us to provide any death certificates or divorce decrees before the ceremony?	
Do you require premarital counseling, classes, or meetings with the celebrant before the wedding? How do we register for them?	
(If you are of different faiths) Are you willing to co-officiate with a celebrant from my fiancé's church or temple?	
Is there a set ceremony format you follow? If we wish, can we design our own vows and choose our own readings? If we do so, how far ahead of the wedding do you need to receive our plans in writing?	

Wedding Site and Celebrant Interview Worksheet

About how long is a typical service?	
Is there space here in the church or temple for the bride to dress? For the groom? May we see the spaces? How early before the wedding can we get into these rooms?	
How early before the wedding can we begin using the church or temple? Is there a ceremony scheduled directly before ours? Directly after?	
Where do couples typically conduct receiving lines? (You may prefer to do so at your reception, but if you have invited guests to your ceremony but not to your reception, you may wish to hold the receiving at your ceremony site.)	
May we provide the music of our choice, or do you have a list of approved musicians and musical selections? Who approves our choices, and how do we submit them?	
Do you have an aisle carpet runner?	

Wedding Site and Celebrant Interview Worksheet	
Is there a church or temple secretary or wedding organizer with whom we should be working?	
Do you have any restrictions on videography/photography inside and outside the building?	
Are there parking restrictions for the bridal party or guests?	
Are there restrictions on what brides and members of the wedding party may wear? (Must women's hair be covered, are sleeveless or bustier gowns permissible, and so on?)	
Do you have restrictions on tossing rice or birdseed?	
Is the site available the night before the wedding for a rehearsal?	

❦ TIP ❦

Your church or temple will have a contact person with whom you make arrangements. Ask that person to name the celebrant's "fee," which is usually not a set number, but an approximate range within which your gift is appropriate.

Getting Ready

Wherever your ceremony is held, you'll need a room where you, your bridesmaids, and your daughters and stepdaughters can dress and a room where your fiancé, his groomsmen, and your sons and stepsons can dress.

Most churches and temples have a "bride's room." Check to be sure that this room fits your space needs (Can two daughters, a bridesmaid, and your mother fit in there?), and check to see what facilities are available for your groom. Grooms are not always so lucky and are often expected to dress in the public rest room. You may prefer to dress at home.

If your ceremony and reception are in a hotel, this dilemma is easily solved. Since you are renting a ballroom space, the hotel may include guest rooms in the fee or, at least, give you a bargain rate on them. Reserve one for the girls, one for the boys, and try to arrange for them to be across the hall or adjacent to each other. Not only will these rooms make for easy prewedding preparations, but they can be convenient respites during the reception if your children and their baby-sitter need a break or a nap. You may even let your children spend your wedding night in one room (with supervision), you and your new husband take the other, and all meet for a breakfast brunch in the hotel restaurant.

To minimize confusion, let everyone involved know who should dress where. And wherever you dress, invite the photographer for great behind-the-scenes shots.

The custom of the bride and groom not seeing each other before the wedding comes from the days of bridal dowries, when families arranged weddings and payments to the groom. The couple were kept apart just in case the groom (who had never seen the bride) didn't like the looks of the bride and jumped ship. This not-so-charming history aside, it can be fun to add anticipation to the wedding day. Even couples who were already living together before the wedding have reported that they enjoyed separating the night before the wedding and seeing each other for the first time at the ceremony.

Seating

If you wish, you may seat guests according to whether they are connected to the bride (on the left) or the groom (on the right, as you face the altar). The ushers ask this question as guests enter. However, since you and your fiancé are both grown-ups and have been for a while now, chances are you have some friends in common who don't want to pick between you. And, if one of you has a large family and the other a small one, you don't want a congregation stuffed into only one side of the church or temple. In that case, instruct your ushers simply to seat people as close to the front as possible and try to distribute them equally on each side of the aisle. If you choose not to use ushers, then people will seat themselves.

Seating your parents

The front pews or rows of chairs are reserved for your parents and your fiancé's parents. If you have children, reserve enough seats for them, too, unless they will be standing up with you during the ceremony.

After all your guests are seated, your fiancé's parents are escorted in and seated on the right. If your fiancé's parents are divorced, they may sit together in the first pew on the right or in the first two pews, if that seems more acceptable to them.

Your mother is escorted in and seated on the left. If your father is not walking you down the aisle, then your father enters with and is seated with your mother. If your parents are divorced, your mother's husband may take his seat with the last guests or may enter with your mother when she is escorted to her seat—your call. If your father is not walking you down the aisle, then he and his new wife may take their seats just before your mother is escorted in. An usher should escort your stepmother to her seat, with your father following behind. Your parents and stepparents may sit together in the first pew on the left or in the first two pews, if you prefer. You can always stick your children in between them, for padding.

If you don't use ushers, it's still thoughtful to make a bit of ceremony over seating the parents. Let the background music end and start special entrance music for the parents. Your fiancé's parents enter and seat themselves first. Then, your parents. If your parents are divorced, your father enters with his new wife, then your mother and her new husband.

If your father escorts you down the aisle, he then takes his seat next to your mother or next to his wife.

$\mathscr{A}$ vote for using ushers

Ushers serve as greeters of your guests and help smooth over that awkward moment of arrival and looking for a seat. If your wedding is in a church or temple, ushers are usually expected. If your ceremony has rows of chairs for seating, ushers can help direct traffic and keep the front seats clear for your parents and children. And if you've got special arrangements for parents, divorced parents, and/or handicapped guests, you'll have prepared your ushers, and they'll be ready to carry out your plans.

The Processional

A second wedding often makes use of nontraditional processionals. You may design your ceremony any way you choose. The placement of aisles, doorways, and seating at your ceremony site will dictate your arrangements, too.

A JEWISH PROCESSIONAL
1. Ushers
2. Bridesmaids
3. Rabbi
4. Best man
5. Groom's mother
6. Groom
7. Groom's father
8. Maid of honor
9. Flower girl
10. Bride's father
11. Bride
12. Bride's mother

⊛ KIDS TALK ⊛

I was my Dad's best man, and I thought it was the coolest!
—*Patrick, 14*

Designing the Ceremony

Involving your children——don't be cute; be sensitive and realistic

Do your children belong in your wedding ceremony? Well, that depends. How steady are your nerves?

At first blush, involving your children in your wedding is a cute idea. Your daughter as your miniature maid of honor. His son as the ring bearer. They could stand at the altar looking cherubic in front of your 250 guests. Or, he could kick the groom in the shin, and she could yell "I hate you!" to your face and run screaming out of the church.

What are your children feeling?

Many children—of all ages—find remarriage to be a pretty confusing time. Even if your divorce or the death of your spouse happened many years ago, your remarriage now can stir up feelings that surprise both you and them.

Your children—whatever their ages—may feel that if they act excited about your wedding, they're somehow being disloyal to Dad. It's not your children's responsibility to adjust their behavior so that you and your fiancé can enjoy your engagement. It's *your* job to understand what they're feeling, how it confuses them, and what kind of support and acceptance they need from you now.

Tread gently when making wedding plans and try to avoid having your children feel left out. No, they don't have to vote on the color of flowers in your bouquet. But they should get a say in the role they'll play in the ceremony and reception and where they will stay during your honeymoon. When a decision involves your children, be sure to gather their input before you finalize anything.

Remember that they are children, not short adults. They

> ### HOW WE DID IT
> My 10-year-old son wanted to carry our rings down the aisle, as long as he didn't have to carry a pillow or walk next to a girl. My daughter walked ahead of me down the aisle carrying flowers, but she didn't want to stand up in front of everyone, so she sat with her grandparents. My eldest son acted as an usher, seating his aunts and uncles, and was happy just to sit in the first row. We let each of them set the tone for their own level of involvement, which made the day easy and relaxed for all of us.
> —*Kathleen, 42*

A CHRISTIAN RECESSIONAL

1. At the end of your ceremony, you and your new husband are the first to walk down the aisle arm in arm and to exit.
2. If you wish, your children can follow you (especially if they are young and would feel most comfortable close by).
3. The flower girl and ring bearer exit as a pair or one after the other.
4. The maid of honor and best man follow.
5. Each bridesmaid meets a groomsman at the center of the altar and exits with him, arm in arm. If you have more or fewer bridesmaids than groomsmen, the bridesmaids exit first, one at a time, followed by the groomsmen, one at a time.

If your wedding is at home or if your ceremony occurs in a site that suits itself to this arrangement, you may skip the recessional and simply turn to face your guests and begin to receive them.

Your faith may have a set processional form that differs from those just mentioned. Your celebrant will be able to tell you what is appropriate for your circumstance.

❧ Don't ❧

❖ Don't force your children into roles in your wedding that they don't want to fill. It will almost surely backfire on you.

❖ Don't feel inhibited by rules. If you want your brother as your "maid of honor" or want to skip the whole processional and just mingle with your guests before the ceremony, do it!

◈ Don't perform music at your own ceremony. If you'd like to serenade your fiancé, or he'd like to play the piano for you, do so at your reception.

◈ RESOURCES ◈

◈ Ask your celebrant and/or church or temple coordinator what interesting readings, songs, and other meaningful gestures they've seen in second weddings. Use their experience!

◈ Check your bookstore for books on writing your own vows. Several collections exist, and one may be right for you.

◈ If you can't think of music selections for the ceremony, ask the musicians you interview to make suggestions.

CHAPTER SEVEN

INVITATIONS,
FLOWERS,
PHOTOGRAPHY, MUSIC

Reserve Your Dates

Once your date and time are settled, start reserving the essentials. If you delay, you may miss out on sites or vendors of your choice. In order of what's the biggest priority to you, reserve:

The florist	____ Reserved wedding date and time	Meeting date: _____
The photographers/ videographers	____ Reserved wedding date and time	Meeting date: _____

The wedding musicians	____ Reserved wedding date and time	Meeting date: _____
The reception band	____ Reserved wedding date and time	Meeting date: _____

Set up meetings with each contact person to discuss the details in a few days or weeks, depending on how much time you have before your wedding.

Invitations

Second-wedding invitations can be traditional or highly imaginative. There's even a company that creates a romance novel–style "cover" customized with your images! (See Resources at end of this chapter.) It's more a matter of your personal style than of rigid social rules, which become more outdated each day. Enjoy yourself, celebrate this event with joy, and don't worry so much.

Style

Stationers stock massive books of literally hundreds of styles of invitations, from formal, classic engraved panel cards to pastel folded cards to die-cut novelty cards. All are completely appropriate for second (and more!) weddings, or consider a custom-designed invitation that suits the two of you (and your children) perfectly.

If your wedding is small, it is appropriate to handwrite

For Kathy and her husband, it was the second wedding for each. Their invitations were simple folded white cards—but the cover was a drawing of a toaster spewing burnt toast! This classic first-wedding symbol—the ubiquitous toaster—became their wedding theme. The centerpieces for their reception tables were toasters holding bouquets of daisies.

invitations, have them written by a calligrapher, or even phone guests and invite them personally.

The most severely traditional invitations are engraved, which is gorgeous, but expensive and rarely done these days, except in the most rarefied social strata. If you like the look of engraving, consider choosing thermography, which is a step above mere printing. Printed invitations, long frowned upon in etiquette manuals, are growing in popularity for second weddings and seem increasingly acceptable. When you consider that handwritten invitations and creative, fun invitations are used for second weddings, what's the big deal about having the invitations printed? A wedding invitation printed on computer paper is tacky, unless you're the future second wife of Bill Gates.

Who issues the invitation?

At first weddings when both your parents are married, your parents are named on the invitations because they'll be hosting the event and footing the bill. At second weddings, couples often host the event themselves. In this case, you don't technically "owe" any parent the honor of having his or her name on your invitations. If your parents volunteer to throw you another wedding, they can certainly be named on your invitations. Or you and your fiancé can be named, without mentioning your parents. If your parents are fighting over who gets to host the wedding, you may choose to have only your and your fiancé's names on the invitation and ask your parents to fund certain aspects of your wedding—one can pay for the cake and another for the liquor, for example. It is also appropriate to name both your parents and their new spouses.

If your parents are separated but not legally divorced, the wording should be as though they are still married and living together.

Sometimes, one parent—like your remarried father or your stepfather—will offer to host your reception. In that case, you may name that person on the reception cards in your invitations:

Mr. Robert Palmer
requests the pleasure of your company
at a dinner and reception
following the wedding of his daughter . . .

Wording

The same stationers' books that display invitations also include wording for a wide array of complicated situations. Look there for ideas, or consider these:

FORMAL AND CLASSIC

This style suits young remarrying couples and brides who are having a bigger wedding styled like a first wedding.

✽

Mr. and Mrs. Bradley Allen Johnson [your parents]
request the honor of your presence
at the marriage of their daughter
Catherine Johnson Timonson
[your current legal name even if it includes your ex's surname]
to
Drew Jeffrey Anderson
[your fiancé's name]
Date
Time
Name of ceremony site
Address of ceremony site

✽

A WEDDING NOT IN A CHURCH

✽

Mr. and Mrs. Bradley Allen Johnson [your parents]
request the pleasure of your company
at the marriage of their daughter . . .

✽

YOU TWO ANNOUNCE

If you feel too old to have your parents announce your wedding or if you and your fiancé are throwing the party or if you just prefer it this way, skip your parents' names.

The honor of your presence
[or "The pleasure of your company"]
is requested at the marriage of
Catherine Johnson Timonson
to
Drew Jeffrey Anderson

❧ ETIQUETTE NOTE ❧

If you want guests to dress in tuxedos and evening gowns, add the phrase "Black tie invited" to the bottom of your invitation.

YOUR MOTHER IS WIDOWED

Mrs. Bradley Johnson
requests the honor of your presence
at the marriage of her daughter
Catherine Johnson Timonson

YOUR MOTHER IS DIVORCED

Mrs. Alicia Johnson
requests the honor of your presence
at the marriage of her daughter
Catherine Johnson Timonson

YOUR MOTHER IS REMARRIED

Mr. and Mrs. Thomas Adams
requests the honour of your presence
at the marriage of her daughter
Catherine Johnson Timonson

IF BOTH SETS OF PARENTS ARE HOSTING THE WEDDING

Mr. and Mrs. Bradley Allen Johnson [your parents]
and
Mr. and Mrs. Jeffrey Anderson [his parents]
request the pleasure of your company
at the marriage of
Catherine Johnson Timonson
and
Drew Jeffrey Anderson

IF YOUR PARENTS AND STEPPARENTS ARE JOINTLY HOSTING THE WEDDING

Mr. and Mrs. Thomas Adams [your mother and stepfather]
and
Mr. and Mrs. Bradley Johnson [your father and stepmother]
request the pleasure of your company
at the marriage of their daughter
Catherine Johnson Timonson

Don't write "No smoking" on your invitations. If you don't want guests to smoke at your reception, don't place ashtrays on the reception tables.

INFORMAL HANDWRITTEN NOTE

Dear Tom and Julie,

    Alex and I will be married at the Whitney Hotel on August 12 at seven-thirty P.M. We hope you will both come to the ceremony and stay for the reception at the hotel.

Love,

Kathy and Alex

FREESTYLE

Your own wording is also appropriate.

Catherine Timonson and Drew Anderson
invite you to share in their joy
as they begin a new life together
Date
Time
Name of ceremony site
Address of ceremony site

or

Our joy will be more complete
if you will share with us
in the ceremony of our marriage
Date
Time
Name of ceremony site
Address of ceremony
and
in the celebration of our reception
Name of reception site
Address of reception
Catherine Johnson Timonson and Drew Jeffrey Anderson

KID FRIENDLY

You can include your children in your invitations. Two examples:

Gretchen and Christopher Timonson
together with
Robert and Steven Anderson
invite you to the marriage of their parents
Catherine Timonson
and
Drew Anderson

or

Catherine Timonson and Drew Anderson
together with their children
request the honor of your presence

Remember, writing "No gifts, please" on your invitation is not appropriate. No mention of gifts or registries should be made in your invitation.

Response cards

It is appropriate to include at the bottom of your invitation: R.S.V.P. or "The honor of a reply is requested." Though including a response card and stamped envelope for guests' replies has long been considered a bit gauche, response cards are becoming more and more popular. It certainly encourages guests to reply more quickly and more accurately, since you preaddress the envelope for the reply. Even strict etiquette mavens nod to the practical considerations of response cards.

☙ ETIQUETTE NOTE ❧

Absolutely, positively, do not print "Cash gifts preferred" or anything like this phrase on your invitations or reception cards. It is simply not polite to refer to gifts of any kind. If you'd prefer cash, mention it to a parent, who may pass the word along—diplomatically, I hope.

At home cards

What is to many first-time brides a quaint and outdated custom has a pragmatic use for an encore bride. At home cards were a way of letting friends and family know when the young couple would return from their honeymoon and be at their new home, ready to receive visitors. For you, however, these cards can send two useful messages: Whether or not you're taking your new husband's name and whether you two are moving into your place, his place, or new digs. Here's how the card is worded:

Catherine Timonson and Drew Anderson
will be at home
after the fifteenth of August
1414 Abercrombie Road
Minneapolis, Minnesota 55443

You may also use this card to let friends and family know where the children will be living:

Catherine Timonson and Drew Anderson
Gretchen and Christopher Timonson
Robert and Steven Anderson
will be at home . . .

Or, use more modern, relaxed wording:

Our new address: 1414 Abercrombie Rd., Minneapolis, MN
Our new family: Catherine Timonson and Drew Anderson. Gretchen
and Chris Timonson. Robert and Steven Anderson.

⊕ TIP ⊛
Add your phone and E-mail address, too.

Reserved pew cards

In a formal or large wedding, you may wish to include a small card called a "reserved pew card" in invitations to family members. These cards are presented to the usher by your guests as a signal to seat them "within the ribbon," in one of the pews reserved with ribbons or flowers. They prevent the faux pas of a close family member being mistakenly seated at the rear of the church.

This custom can have a special application if you have any sticky situations with divorced parents. Number the cards to match the pew numbers and ask the ushers to seat guests accordingly. This way, you can avoid seating your mother next to your father's new wife.

Sample wording:

Pew 2 Bride's reserved section
Mr. and Mrs. Alex Marx
Please present this card to the usher

If your wedding is small, you can simply speak to your family and guests and let them know where you'd like them to sit.

Extra enclosures

Guests appreciate such helps as maps to the church and reception, lists of nearby hotels, and even wordier explanations of what will be going on at your wedding and reception. Producing such a sheet on your computer is fine, just print it up on decent paper, fold it, and insert it in your invitation envelope.

Guests from out of town may appreciate information about your town, sites to see, and things to do. You may send this information in a separate mailing to specific guests. Folding up a brochure on an amusement park and stuffing it into your invitation is not dignified.

You may also send a "visitor's packet" as a follow-up to your formal invitation.

❧ ETIQUETTE NOTE ❧

"No children allowed." Though that may be your wish, you can't print it on your invitation or reception card. Instead, address your outer and inner invitation only to the adults in the family. This will send the message to most guests. Also communicate your wishes to your family, who will help spread the word. If both you and your fiancé have children, guests may assume that their children are also welcome. They shouldn't, but they might.

Inner and outer envelopes

Any style of invitation may use both an inner and outer envelope. The outer envelope is addressed for the postal service; the inner envelope lists the specific guests invited. Using inner envelopes can be helpful if you wish to make it clear that children are not invited. For example, the outer envelope would read "Mr. and Mrs. Edward Erickson" and the inner envelope would read "Mr. and Mrs. Erickson." If you want to invite children, write "Mr. and Mrs. Erickson" and underneath "Heather and Steven." I've received many wedding invitations with our first names written on the inside envelope—"Pamela

Hill Nettleton and William Henry Schrickel" or even "Pam and Bill"—and thought that was personal and warm. Also, given the fact that I've been married four times, Bill has been married three times, and we are raising three children with two different last names, every now and then someone gets confused and refers to Bill as "Mr. Nettleton" or me as "Mrs. Schrickel." None of these understandable errors raises our blood pressure, for Pete's sake, and shouldn't raise yours or your friends'. We're just glad to be asked to the party!

Ordering invitations

Order enough invitations to send keepsake copies to your parents, his parents, and your children. Each of your children should receive an invitation of his or her own. Order extras for surprises—"Oh gosh, we forgot Bob and Amy!"—and extra envelopes in case you make a mistake in addressing them. Order invitations once the date, place, and time for your ceremony and reception are set. Allow enough time for printing, addressing, and mailing. Plan for guests to receive your invitations four to eight weeks before your wedding. If your wedding involves an out-of-town trip for which guests must plan, send invitations even earlier.

❧ TIP ❧

If you wish, you can purchase romantic stamps—ones with "Love" or hearts on them—from the post office for your invitations. Visit your post office and ask what's available. Maybe someday they'll invent a "Love Again" stamp!

Wedding announcements

You may wish to send out announcements of your wedding, especially if your ceremony is small or private. These announcements are always sent *after* your wedding, and only to people you did not invite to your ceremony and reception. Those who receive announcements are not bound to reply with a card or gift, though they may if they choose. The wording is similar to the wording on your invitation, though instead of "the pleasure of your company" or the "the honor of your presence," you'll say "announce the marriage of."

Mr. and Mrs. Bradley Allen Johnson [your parents]
announce the marriage of
Catherine Johnson Timonson
to
Drew Jeffrey Anderson
Date
Time
Name of ceremony site
Address of ceremony site

or

Catherine Johnson Timonson
and
Drew Jeffrey Anderson
announce their marriage . . .

Your Wedding Flowers

Flowers add drama, romance, and a heady scent to your wedding day. The only second-time floral no-no seems to be orange blossoms, viewed by many as a sign of virginity.

What flowers do you need?

❖ A bouquet for you. If you prefer, you can carry a white Bible or prayer book. If you choose your gown at a bridal salon, ask your sales consultant for advice about what type of bouquet best suits your dress. Some salons even have silk flower bouquets in various sizes and configurations for you to try with your gown.

❖ Bouquets for your bridesmaids

❖ A basket of flowers or petals for the flower girl

❖ Hair ornaments for you and your bridesmaids, if you wish to wear flowers

❖ A boutonniere for your groom

❖ Boutonnieres for groomsmen and ushers

❖ Your children and stepchildren will feel grown-up wearing boutonnieres on their jackets and carrying bouquets. Even if they don't want to give speeches during the wedding, they'll enjoy being singled out as "family" by wearing or carrying flowers. Tell your florist which flowers are for the children, so the arrangements will be sized appropriately.

❖ Corsages for your mothers and stepmothers

- Boutonnieres for your fathers and stepfathers

- Corsages and boutonnieres for your grandparents, if you wish

- If you have asked friends or family members to perform special tasks, such as asking guests to sign the guest book or helping you dress, you may give them corsages or boutonnieres. These flowers are optional and should be smaller and less important than the flowers for your wedding party, your children, and your parents.

- Ceremony site decorations. If your ceremony is at a church or temple, visit it (and photograph it for the florist) to see which are logical places for floral displays. If your ceremony is in a hotel or other site that doesn't have an altar or clear focal point, a candelabra decorated with flowers, an arbor, a canopy, or even a large bouquet can help "mark" where the ceremony will occur (and will look better than a blank wall in photos). Work with your florist to choose ceremony flowers that can do double-duty at the reception.

- Reserved pew markers. If you are holding the first pew or two for your children and/or family members, mark the end of the pew with flowers. A white satin bow on the end chair or end of the pew is fine, too.

- Reception decorations. The ceremony flowers can be moved to stand at the entrance to your reception site, "frame" the bride's table, or placed elsewhere. Ask your florist to show you photos of other receptions for more decoration ideas.

- Wedding cake table decorations. Fresh flowers can be placed on your wedding cake, loose flowers and greens can be placed on the tablecloth, and flowers and/or ribbon can be placed on the ceremonial cake-cutting knife.

- If you wish, flowers and/or ribbon can be placed on the champagne toasting glasses. Make them small, or you won't be able to hold the stems of the glasses.

- Table centerpieces. Some of your ceremony flowers may be used as serving-table accents. Guest-table centerpieces can be flowers, flowers and candles, just candles, or other items.

- A going-away corsage for you, if you want one. Warning: Depending on your age, you run the risk of a well-meaning hotel clerk asking you if your *daughter* just got married.

Your bouquet

Ask your florist for advice about what sort of bouquet would flatter you and fit your dress. If possible, show the florist a photo of your gown. If your dress is street length, you won't want a cascading bouquet that trails below the hem of your dress. If your gown is full skirted and voluminous, you won't want a tiny sprig of flowers. Your bouquet should be in proportion to what you are wearing.

Ask your florist to make your bouquet easy for you to carry by wrapping the flower stems with ribbon and creating a "handle." For my last wedding, I wanted a simple, gathered bouquet of purple hydrangea, stock, and roses, tied with a ribbon. The flowers were gorgeous, but I hadn't thought about how thick those stems would be, gathered together. Carrying that bundle around all day was carpal tunnel—inducing. (Also, be sure to dry off the stems of your bouquet before you carry it, or you'll get water spots on your dress.)

There are no color rules for second brides.

Other Florist Services

Some florists can rent for you or provide their own candelabras, arbors, canopies, aisle runners, and other features that can add to your ceremony.

If your church or ceremony site is large, but your guest list is small, consult with your florist to help make the space appear and feel more intimate. Adjust the lighting in the room to focus on the area of the ceremony and leave the larger, empty pews dark. Group flowers around the occupied pews to "frame" the area you're using.

Reception table and room-decorating ideas

Use your imagination—and the imagination of your florist.

Possibilities:

- Arches of balloons, ivy, or flowers

- Tree branches and ivy sprigs worked into the ceiling

- Swaths of fabric draped above windows and from the ceiling

- Tiny twinkle lights and tulle wrapped around the tent or canopy legs

- Strings of lanterns, used indoors or outdoors
- Pottery bowls or cornucopias filled with harvest produce
- Portable columns placed at the entry
- Topiaries or small trees on tabletops
- Floating candles or flowers in the pool

Who pays?

Traditionally, the groom pays *at least* for your bouquet and often for corsages for the mothers and grandmothers and boutonnieres for himself, his groomsmen, and ushers. He may also pay for the rest of the flowers if he wishes. At second weddings, both the bride and groom often share expenses equally, so this may be a moot issue. If either of your parents want to help with expenses, they may want to pay for the church decorations or table centerpieces. Don't ask your parents to pay for their own corsages!

HOW WE DID IT

We didn't want a feeling of being overwhelmed by flowers, but we wanted their fragrance and that sense of freshness and occasion you get from floral arrangements. So we chose just one type of flower, my favorite, daisies, and used them everywhere. Big bunches of daises on tables, on the altar, in bouquets. It was a one-note floral display, but I thought it was simple and elegant.

—*Cathy, 43*

Flower delivery

This is a trickier point than you may think. If you're taking photos before your ceremony, you'll need the flowers early. If the photo session is hours before the wedding and any of the photos are taken outdoors in strong sunshine or heat, you may have to dampen the flowers periodically or refrigerate them (ask your florist what is best for your type of flowers). If your wedding bouquet is not very expensive, consider ordering two, to be sure your ceremony bouquet is fresh and pretty. Ask a friend or the site coordinator to help you keep bouquets fresh by providing vases of water and a towel (don't let wet flowers drip on your dress).

If your flowers are being delivered to your home, appoint someone to look for them and call the florist if they are late. Ahead of time, clear space in the refrigerator (if your florist has advised refrigeration). Tall bouquets can take up a lot of refrigerator space that is probably already at a minimum with food for the reception. Alert a neighbor to your possible need for emergency refrigeration!

If your flowers are being delivered to the church or temple, ask the church which door the florist should use. Appoint someone to wait there for the flowers, call the florist if the flowers don't arrive on schedule, and place the flowers where you want them when they arrive. If you need refrigeration or water, ask the church or temple what facilities are available to you.

The flowers for your reception should be delivered directly to that site, in enough time to arrange them on the tables. Designate a person at that site to receive and place the flowers. If your reception is at home, ask the florist for tips on how to make sure your flowers stay fresh. This is another reason, if you are having a home wedding, that you *must* have at least one person at home attending to details while you're off at your wedding.

❧ KIDS TALK ❧

I got my very own bouquet!
—*Emmie, 5*

Florist Interview Worksheet

What type of flowers are in season and affordable at the time of our wedding?	
Can you show us photographs of past wedding arrangements and bouquets you've done?	
Have you ever done weddings at our wedding site and reception site before? Do you have photos of what you did there? What would you suggest?	
When can flowers be delivered?	
(If you are having fresh flowers on the wedding cake and/or cake table) Will you arrange the cake flowers, or do you want the caterer to do it?	
Do you just deliver the flowers, or will you place them?	
Are you willing to make one delivery to the wedding site and another to the reception site?	

Florist Interview Worksheet

Do you have any special instructions for how we can keep the flowers fresh throughout the day?	
Do you need a down payment?	
When is the full payment due?	
Do we need to make arrangements to return the vases to you, or are those included in our price?	
How can I preserve my wedding bouquet?	

Budget stretchers

◆ Choose flowers that are plentiful and easily obtained in your area at the time of year of your wedding. Out-of-season flowers that have to be flown in from a tropical clime or far-away greenhouse add to your cost exponentially.

◆ Ask the florist if a particular color of flower is less expensive than another.

◆ If there is a wedding before or after yours in the church, talk to that bride about the two of you sharing the cost of altar and church decorations.

◆ Ask the florist to show you examples of inexpensive but beautiful flowers—you may find you can easily give up roses for larkspur or stock!

◆ Choose inexpensive "filler" flowers for church decorations and bouquets and use more expensive flowers, like orchids or roses, as accents.

◆ Not every decoration and centerpiece has to be flowers. A church pew can be reserved with a satin ribbon. Table centerpieces can be rented candelabras, collections of framed photos, a striking garden ornament, or something of special meaning to you and your fiancé. Reception decorations can include balloons, streamers, ribbons, confetti—almost anything.

◆ Instead of using arranged bouquets, simply lay or scatter blooms and/or petals on tables. Two or three stalks of gladiolas laid across a table are striking, as are scattered petals over a white tablecloth.

will look terrific photographed in black and white. And if your photographer happens to snap your 9-year-old son dancing with your 70-year-old mother at your reception, you'll have a family heirloom photograph.

What do you want photographed?

Talk with your fiancé about your priorities for photography and videography. Some couples want absolutely everything recorded. Others want only certain special moments and family shots. Do you want more shots of your wedding ceremony or more of your guests at the reception? Try to imagine what you'll want to look back on and remember. You may not want forty-two photographs of you in your dress at the center of everything as much as you'll want photos of your children, your guests, and your party.

It is increasingly common for couples and their wedding parties to spend an hour or more *before* the wedding having group shots taken. This practice helps avoid long delays between the ceremony and the reception, but it also means that you'll lose the special moment when the groom sees you for the first time as you begin your walk down the aisle. A

HOW WE DID IT

At our wedding, our photographer suggested that we shoot one photo of all our wedding guests. We lined everybody up on the hotel's wide staircase for a terrific photo of just about everyone in the world we care about. After the wedding, we had reprints made and sent one out with each thank-you note.

—*Eddie, 42*

---

compromise could be to have as many photos as possible taken before the wedding that don't include both you and your fiancé (you and your parents, him and his parents, you and your children, him and his children, you and your brides-maids, and so on).

❧ Tip ❧

Some photographers have printed lists of common wedding photos. Ask for one and check off the shots you want.

Call early

Top wedding photographers and videographers book far ahead. Ask friends for recommendations and call early! Visit the photographer before you book a date. Look at samples to see if the photos have the quality and spirit that you want, then call past clients to see if the photographer handles ceremonies and receptions in a polite, easygoing, friendly manner. Ask if the photographer manages to blend into the background or takes center stage.

Make a list of the moments you want recorded and share them with the photographer when you meet. Talk frankly about how much time all these shots will take. More than one bride has missed much of her own reception because she had to pose for photos. Decide when it will be most convenient to take photos and a video and work with the photographer/videographer to set a schedule. The timing of your photos/videos can affect the pacing of your entire day. A reliable, competent photographer can give you the benefit of his or her experience and make suggestions about how events can best be recorded without interrupting your wedding.

At my first wedding, a self-centered photographer was so eager to leave for his vacation that he rushed our wedding party into photos on the altar before we could hold our receiving line, which forced us to have our photos taken with all the guests seated, watching us. It went against everything he and I had agreed to ahead of time, and it still makes me angry to think about it!

This *is* a great chance to record a moment when you, your new spouse, and all your children are showered, nicely dressed, and happy at the same time. But you may wish to go light on the formal, posed photos and ask your photographer/videographer to capture what's naturally happening in more candid shots. Also, don't forget to ask your photographer to get shots of each guest table—your guests are an important part of your happy memories of this day, and you'll want to remember who was there with you.

Do record the event, don't interrupt it

Do ask the photographer/videographer to be as discreet as possible. You don't want her hanging over the altar railing to get a good angle or interrupting your first married kiss because she wants better lighting. You may even wish to restrict certain moments in your religious ceremony from being photographed. Remember that some religions or religious wedding sites forbid the use of flash photography or any photography.

Photographer/Videographer Interview Worksheet

Do you work in black and white, color, or both?	
How many hours do you spend with clients?	
Are you willing to come to our house to take "getting ready" shots, go to the church for wedding shots, and then go to the reception for shots there?	
Do you have a set number of photos you take?	
Can we give you a list of special photos we want?	
Can you talk us through a typical wedding schedule for you? When do you start and finish?	
Can we buy whatever photographs we want, or must we purchase certain packages?	
What are your prices? (Get this in writing.)	

Photographer/Videographer Interview Worksheet

Do you require a down payment?	
When can we see proofs?	
How many proofs do we get?	
How long can we keep proofs?	
Do you supply albums, or do we buy those ourselves?	
Will *you* be our photographer, or will your studio send someone else?	
Do you dress like a wedding guest when you work? (A photographer in jeans can be unseemly.)	
Do you provide unedited tapes or do you produce a "best-moments" tape?	
Do you use one or two cameras?	
Are the cameras stationary or mobile?	

Budget-stretching tips

- Provide your own wedding album, purchased at a good-quality stationery store.

- Minimize the number of 8 × 10 and other enlargements and instead order 3 × 5 or 4 × 5 prints.

- Ask if, instead of proofs, your photographer could provide 3 × 5 prints that you could keep. These prints may cost slightly more, but they may allow you to order fewer enlargements.

- Limit the professional photographer to portraits of the family and wedding party before or after the wedding and ask friends to take snapshots of everything else.

- Cut the photographer's hours to a minimum. Instead of taking "getting ready" shots, portraits before the wedding, shots during the wedding, shots during the reception, and shots as you leave, see if you can narrow the time to the essentials: wedding photos, reception photos, portraits in between.

❖ KIDS TALK ❖

The guy who did the video for my dad's wedding interviewed each of us kids about what it felt like to see our parents getting married. That was neat, and when we watch that video, it always makes my dad laugh.

—Tim, 11

Music

If you, your mother, and your best friend from grade school are going to cry, it will be while music is playing. Music is the soul of a romantic wedding and a way that you and your fiancé can express your personalities and style. Start writing down names of songs and pieces that you especially like—and find the sheet music! Vocalists, organists and musicians will likely need sheet music for any special requests that aren't common "wedding" themes, and it can be hard to find.

Hint: buying sheet music of songs you want sung lets you carefully check the lyrics for phrases that would be unseemly or hilarious during a wedding. A college friend had a romantic Elvis tune sung at her wedding, but only halfway down the aisle realized that the words had special and bizarre meaning during a wedding: "Wise men say only fools rush in but I can't help falling in love with you . . ."

What music will you need?

FOR YOUR CEREMONY

❖ "Background" instrumental music played on an organ or other instruments before the wedding while guests are arriving and being seated. These selections may need to be approved by your celebrant, who may also be able to give you a list of appropriate choices. Classical selections and hymns are good pieces to begin with; some standard love songs may also be allowed. Good instruments: strings, a harp, an organ, a piano, and a flute.

❖ A special instrumental piece for seating your mother, your fiancé's parents, and your children, if they are not in the wedding party

- Your processional. Good instruments and music: an organ, a trumpet, something stirring and less soft.

- A special song or two played during the ceremony. Rather than choose a time when everything in the ceremony stops for the song, place the song at a time when the celebrant is occupied and the congregation would normally be praying or singing.

- Your recessional. Good instruments and music: an organ, a trumpet, something triumphant and joyful.

- Background music played during your receiving line and/or as guests disperse. Ask the musicians to continue to play until the last guest has left the building. Good instruments: an organ, strings, a harp, a piano, a flute, or a guitar.

FOR YOUR RECEPTION

- Background music for your receiving line and as guests arrive. This music should be soft enough to be easily spoken and heard over.

- If you have musicians present, ask for a soft drum roll or other musical "announcement" for cake cutting and champagne toasting.

- If you're having dancing, choose special music for your first dance with your new husband. This music can be "your song," or a romantic tune. Traditionally, your family and wedding party eventually join you two in this dance, so something your parents can dance to is a good idea. Heavy metal rock music is not.

- If you're having dancing, choose dance music. You need not select every song, but if you and your fiancé have favorites, be sure to give the band a list.

- Last dance song

Ceremony music

At your church or temple interview, you'll determine what kind of music is allowed and whether a church organist is available. If one is available, arrange to listen to his or her playing during a service or wedding (you needn't crash a stranger's wedding; just stand in the hall long enough to hear the quality of musicianship). If you like the organist, engage him or her. If not, engage your own.

Discuss with your celebrant the best times during the service for music to be played and/or sung. Furnish your celebrant with a list of your selections well ahead of time. If any song is going to be rejected, it's best to find out early and make another choice.

Pay your ceremony musicians before the wedding or set aside a check in a labeled envelope and give it to a trustworthy person, like the best man, to pay the musicians after the ceremony.

Musician Interview Worksheet

Do you know and/or specialize in the type of music we want to hear? (Have a list of several favorite selections as examples.)	
(Name the selections you absolutely must have.) Do you need us to provide you with sheet music for these songs?	
Can we obtain an audition tape or go to a live performance to hear and see you?	
Will the musicians we listened to in person or on the tape be *the* musicians who play at our wedding? Do you ever hire substitutes? (Specify in writing that you won't accept substitutes.)	
What do you wear when you play? (Let the band know how you and your wedding party will be dressed and ask them to fit in.)	

Reception music

Choose your party music to match your wedding style. If you're having a 1940s theme wedding, choose Sinatra standards and romantic crooner tunes. If you love to boogie, hire a rock band (your children will love it, your parents probably won't!). Of course, you can mix styles—soft instrumentals during dinner, rock and roll for the dance.

The key to being pleased with the music at your wedding is this: Don't hire musicians you haven't heard. Get recommendations from friends or track down bands you've heard and liked. Hear the band play at another gig or take home an audition tape. Then meet with the band for an interview.

Your reception musicians may require a down payment before your reception and may require payment in cash or a check at the end of your party. If so, make out the checks (or get cash) ahead of time and give it to the best man to pay the band for you.

Budget stretchers

- Rather than pay professional musicians to play for your entire reception, save them for the dance (if you have one). A single instrument, like a classical guitar or a harp, can provide elegant music during the receiving line and dinner.

- Use cassette tapes or CDs during the receiving line and dinner portion of your reception.

❧ Bridal salons and wedding-supply shops carry many helpful items, including lists of appropriate wedding music and sheet music.

❧ Bridal magazines can be tremendous resources—especially the ads, which may be advertising exactly the products you are looking for!

❧ Don't wonder how to handle second-wedding issues in silence. Ask florists, musicians, caterers, and other vendors you interview for ideas and input. They do weddings for a living—they've probably seen more second (and third, and fourth) weddings in the past month than you'll see in a lifetime.

❧ For romance novel–style invitations, contact:

> Custom Romance
> 2318 Milwaukee Avenue
> Minneapolis, MN 55404
> 866-890-1315
> www.customromance.com

CHAPTER EIGHT

RECEPTION, CATERERS, AND CAKE

Reserve Your Dates

When you know your wedding date and time, check with reception sites and caterers for availability. Make appointments with available sites and vendors and reserve:

The reception site	____ Reserved wedding date and time	Meeting date: _____
The caterer	____ Reserved wedding date and time	Meeting date: _____

Set up meetings with each contact person to discuss the details in a few days or weeks, depending on how much time you have before your wedding.

After you determine the size of your guest list, you can choose a wedding site and reception site. Caterers advise that about one-fourth of your invited guests will be unable to attend, so for rough planning purposes now, use that figure as your guide. Once you've received all your R.S.V.P.s, you'll want to confirm exact counts with your site and your caterer.

Finding a Reception Site

As an encore bride, you've probably thrown a few terrific parties since your last wedding. All that experience will make planning this reception easier and more fun. Now you know what you like, know the kinds of events you like to attend, and know what works when you entertain. Put all that knowledge to use in planning a terrific after-wedding party.

To start a list of likely sites, check with your bridal salon and your caterer (if you already know one), and try the yellow pages. Also, if your city has a local bridal newsletter or publication, it may include a guide to area hotels, clubs, and other reception sites.

Receptions can be held in a limitless variety of places. Let the number of guests and the style of reception that you and your fiancé prefer act as your guide. For a small wedding, consider renting a bed-and-breakfast for the ceremony, reception, and honeymoon. If your city has a historic district of grand old homes, investigate whether any can be rented for special occasions. Historic buildings, like courthouses and old libraries, sometimes rent extraordinary spaces that accommodate large crowds. Country clubs, hotels, halls, church basements, your own home, a local park, conservatories, museums, aquariums, and private clubs are more possibilities.

Go back to your wedding style worksheet. The questions you and your fiancé answered should help you decide where your reception should be.

If you have children, their involvement may help drive your decision. If they are young, you may wish to choose an informal site where children (and childish behavior) are welcome. A reception site near your home makes it easier for you to hire a baby-sitter to watch your children and even take them home if they get tired or cranky.

Visit in person

If you're having arguments about where to hold the reception, table the discussion for a short while and visit some actual sites. Seeing what is available may help both of you visualize your wedding more accurately. Your fiancé could be against using a hotel because he envisions the tacky hotel meeting room his company uses; when he sees the elegant ballroom at a top hotel on your list, he may be swayed. You could be worried about holding your reception at the country club because you don't like its chef—but if you visit, you may discover that you can bring in your own caterer.

Make a list of potential sites, drive by them to rule out ones that aren't right from the outside, then phone the others and schedule appointments to tour the facilities. When you call, ask if someone will have time to sit down with you and answer your questions. In some cases, a site representative may give you some printed information about rates and ask you to call a special-event coordinator later.

Use the reception site worksheet as a guide when you visit

each site. It lists most of the questions you'll need answered, including questions about catering, menus, rates, parking, and more.

Check out the right time of day

If you can, visit—or at least drive by—potential sites at the same time of day when you'd like to hold your reception. What looks like a quiet part of town with lots of parking in the evening may be heavily trafficked during the day. What looks shabby during the day may look elegant by soft candlelight. If you've got a year to plan, see your site on the same day this year that will be your wedding date next year. This is an especially useful idea if you are having your reception outdoors. You'll be able to see how the plantings and gardens look at the exact time of year when you'll be married.

When setting the time of your reception, remember your children. Choose a time of day when they'll be at their best. If you schedule your reception to start at the hour when your youngest needs her nap, you're asking for trouble.

If Your Reception Is at Home

Early in your planning, visit a shop that specializes in rentals for weddings. Ask for suggestions for home weddings. The shop will have items on display and even more items available by special order that you may not otherwise imagine—extra-large grills, champagne coolers, romantic tents, strings of outdoor lights, and so on. Plan for both good weather and bad (a tent can keep a rain shower from ruining your reception; portable heaters can keep guests from flocking into the house if it is cold). Keep the traffic flowing by setting up various food and drink stations around the house. Have guests sign the guest book on a stair landing, serve punch and coffee on the porch, set up the bar in the living room, put the food in the dining room.

Think creatively. If your living and dining room aren't large enough spaces for all your guests, transform your garage into another gathering space. Cover the walls with sheets or fabric, throw rugs on the floor, and bring in the flowers!

A Restaurant Reception

If your wedding is small enough (and a favorite restaurant is large enough) consider holding your reception in a private room or renting the restaurant. If it's a small-enough ceremony and your budget can stand it, guests could order from the menu. Add champagne for the group and have a wedding cake, even a small one, delivered.

A Delayed Reception

If your ceremony was held out of town or was private, you may wish to schedule a reception or party days or weeks after your actual wedding day. You need not wear your wedding dress (unless you want to), and a receiving line is optional.

Reception Site Worksheet

What is your formal address? (You'll need it for your invitations.)	
Who will be our contact person for questions and arrangements?	
What sort of wedding packages do you offer?	
Do your ballrooms rent by the hour or evening?	
Will there be another event scheduled just before or after ours?	
Must we use your caterer and menu, or may we bring in our own?	
Must we work off your established menu, or may we make special requests?	
Once we choose a menu, could we ask the chef to make it, and could we sample it ahead of time?	

Are tables, chairs, linens, china, and crystal all included in your charges, or are they extra?	
How many staff will you provide to serve, direct guests, tend bar, and so forth? If we want extra help, can we have it if we're willing to pay for it?	
Can we see your china and serving pieces? (If you want silver and the site uses plastic, you'll want to know.)	
Do you have a silver service for coffee and tea?	
Do you have a punchbowl and enough glass cups?	
How do you structure charging for liquor?	
Are gratuities for the staff included in your fee?	

Reception Site Worksheet

How much parking is available near you? Will the guests have to pay a fee? Can we arrange for valet parking?	
Where can the band and other musicians set up?	
Do you have a sound system that the band/musicians can use?	
When the band is on a break, do you have a system over which we can play tapes/CDs?	
Is there a cloakroom available for guests?	
Do you allow photography and videography? (Cables and lighting can disturb some sites.)	

Consider a Caterer

A caterer works with you to plan a menu; prepares and cooks the food; decides the best way and time to serve the food; helps coordinate flowers and decorating; and can provide any needed serving pieces, linens, tables, and chairs. A caterer also provides waitstaff and bartenders and cleans up after your reception. Some of these services may be available from your caterer but cost extra. Some of these services may be available at no extra cost from your site.

Perhaps the most important thing a caterer can offer you is experience. An experienced caterer has worked hundreds of parties, receptions, and special events. This expertise is valuable. With a caterer, you've got an expert in traffic flow (where to place buffet tables, the bar, and the receiving line), what kinds of foods are the most popular with guests, how much of which kinds of foods to order, and more.

If you are having a home reception, hiring a caterer is the only way you are going to be able to relax and enjoy your guests and the day. Plus, if you have children, you'll be both bride and Mommy. Give yourself a break and get help with preparing and serving your meal.

Some reception sites provide their own caterer and serving staff. Before you choose one of these sites, eat dinner there. There's no better way to judge the quality of the food and service staff. Some sites even offer one free meal to you and your fiancé so you can sample their wares.

Other sites have a list of outside caterers they will work with. Before you commit to one of those sites, check out the caterers first. You don't want to fall in love with a site and get stuck with the wrong caterer.

If you know and like a caterer you've used before (lucky you!), limit your list to sites that allow you to bring in the caterer of your choice.

Budgeting for a caterer

The food you serve is probably the most expensive part of your entire wedding—whether you use a private caterer or the chef at your reception site. If you haven't used a caterer before, you may be concerned that the cost will be too much.

However, it *is* possible to find catering services in a range of prices, from high-end society caterers to freelance chefs.

The "extra" services that many caterers provide—decorations, centerpieces, flowers, coordinating the event, overseeing other details—sometimes cost extra, but are sometimes part of the package. To save money, choose a site that provides tables, chairs, linens, and serving pieces and use the caterer only for cooking and serving. Or if your priority is to have the reception run smoothly without you having to check on details yourself, then everything a caterer can do to help will be welcome.

A caterer will provide you with a proposal menu and an estimate. You can adjust the menu until it suits your budget. Then, you'll get a written final estimate. Depending on the custom where you live, you'll likely be asked to pay a large advance and to pay the rest after the reception. Some sites and some caterers may want payment before you and your groom leave. If possible, arrange with the best man to handle this task for you.

Choosing a caterer

Start with recommendations from friends. Call your favorite restaurant and see if it caters special events—many do. Bridal salons and wedding consultants will have recommendations, too.

Whether you are choosing a catering service on its own or are working with a caterer linked to your site, you'll need to evaluate the quality of service you're likely to get at your reception. Probably the best way to do so is to have attended a previous event there. So think: Have you attended a well-run, beautifully served wedding, dinner, bar mitzvah, or company event? That's a good starting place. The next best thing:

Ask friends for recommendations. Or, look through the caterer's book of photos of past events and then call some of his or her past clients.

Remember: With a caterer, you are judging the presentation and quality of the food, but you are also looking for organization, enthusiasm about helping you coordinate flowers and decorations (if you want this additional help), and guest-friendly service. Choose a caterer who shares your sense of fun and expectation about this event. Choose a caterer who will also work with you to create a children's menu and help decorate in kid-friendly ways. If you don't think you can work well together, keep looking for another caterer.

Working with a caterer

Whether your caterer is on staff at your reception site or is a private caterer you've hired, you'll need to work together to plan a menu and finalize details. Think about your friends and family, and your and your fiancé's style, and communicate the feeling of your wedding and your reception to your caterer. He or she can then suggest several menus to fit your guests and your style. Unless your caterer thinks he's a genius and gets touchy about being challenged (why did you choose *this* guy?), you should

HOW WE DID IT
Ask for recommendations from friends and family, but use your own judgment. My fiancé and I went to *the* society catering service and found it uncooperative and snooty. We found a smaller shop that really went out of its way to help us. We got so many extra touches that we would never have thought of ourselves, and we sure wouldn't have gotten them from the well-known caterer that we thought we'd be using.
—*Nancy, 52*

Caterer Interview Worksheet

Do you have wedding packages?	
Have you worked at our reception site before?	
Can you show us sample menus of past events you've catered?	
Do you provide only menu planning and food services, or can you also help with flowers, decorations, overseeing the reception, and other things? Are these things included in your estimate? If they are extra, could you list them as line items?	
Can we see your china and serving pieces? (If you want silver and the caterer uses plastic, you'll want to know.)	
Do you have a silver service for coffee and tea?	
Do you have a punchbowl and enough glass cups?	

Caterer Interview Worksheet

Will you check with our reception site to coordinate if we need to rent additional tables, chairs, linens, china, and serving pieces? Will that all be an extra charge, or are some of these items included in your charges?

If there is an emergency and we need to cancel or postpone the wedding, what is your policy? How much notice do you need? Can our deposit be returned?

Do you have a time limit on how long you will stay during the reception? Can your staff stay until our guests are gone and we're ready to end the reception? (You don't want to end your reception earlier than you wanted to because the caterers had to leave!)

Do you provide the cake? Do you work with special bakers? Can we supply our own cake if we wish? Are there any bakers you would recommend?

How many menu proposals will you give us? Will you keep working with us until we get a menu we all like?	
Are gratuities included in your fee?	

be able to go back and forth a bit about menu items until you've got something you all like.

Your Menu

Let your personal style and the time of day of your wedding determine your menu. You may want a reception theme: If you two met at an Italian restaurant and have gone back there every Friday night since, celebrate your romantic spirit by throwing red-checkered cloths over the tables and serving a meal of Tuscan abundance in earthenware bowls and platters, with biscotti served with coffee for dessert. Or you may just want an elegant, simple reception. The time of day dictates some menu and formality choices. Remember to add choices that your children will enjoy and actually eat!

❧ TIP ❦

Don't invite your guests to a dinner-time wedding and then try to save money by serving only a few canapés. The time of your ceremony will tell your guests what kind of refreshments to expect. Rather than stint on your menu, choose a time of day your budget can handle, and do a simple menu well and with style.

Wedding breakfast

If your wedding is in the morning, your reception can be a breakfast (even if it's served as late as lunchtime). Offer a buffet that includes traditional breakfast foods plus lunch entrées, styled after hotel breakfast buffets of eggs, crepes, fruit, pastries, roast beef, and salads. Or serve your guests two or three courses at their tables.

Wedding tea

If your wedding is in the afternoon, guests will not expect a meal. A wedding tea keeps your costs down and is a good option on a budget. Your tea menu may be as simple or elaborate as you wish: small open-faced sandwiches, cold canapés, punch, and coffee or an elegant high tea, with each table receiving the traditional three-tiered plates of canapés and miniature desserts.

Wedding cocktails

If your wedding is in the afternoon, but tea seems too staid for you, an elegant option is a cocktail party. Your caterers can pass hot and cold appetizers on trays, an open bar can serve martinis and other cocktails, and your cake can be served with espresso.

Wedding dinner

If your wedding is in the evening, your guests will expect dinner. It can be served to each table or be a buffet.

Wedding Cake

Some caterers bake and provide wedding cakes, others work with bakeries, and some prefer to have you provide your own cake. A traditional white cake frosted in white and layered in tiers is appropriate for any wedding—it's not just for first-timers. However, you and your fiancé can also use your imagination and serve your favorite dessert.

Gone are the days when wedding cakes had to be white—especially for encore brides. Your color scheme can be reflected in the frosting and/or filling. Or you can choose an all-white cake and decorate the cake and the table with fresh flowers. Your cake should reflect the feeling you're trying to create with your wedding and reception. A meticulously decorated and detailed high-tiered cake reflects a formal atmosphere. A smaller cake surrounded with garden flowers imparts a more relaxed, family feeling.

And you don't *have* to have

> **HOW WE DID IT**
> We had an excellent, three-course gourmet meal served at each table. But we're also crazy about candy—it's our downfall!—so we had a silver bowl of M&Ms sitting by each centerpiece.
> —*Andi and Calvin, 30 and 30*

cake. Brides have chosen other desserts, too. Glass-footed cake plates can be stacked into tiers and arranged with miniature pies, pastries, or petit fours, or elegant tortes and layered pastries can be served on silver trays.

One encore bride I know had two miniature wedding cakes made for her two children. They looked like fancy, tiered cupcakes, and the children loved them!

Investigate the bakeries in your area to discover which ones specialize in wedding cakes or ask your caterer for a list of possibilities. If you've seen and eaten terrific cake at a wedding or a party, your investigative work is half done. Visit two or three bakeries and look through their photo albums of cake styles. If you've seen a magazine photo of a cake that you like, show it to your pastry chef and ask if she can produce that cake.

Prices for cakes can vary widely, so ask. Cakes are typically priced per serving, but serving sizes may vary, too. It's perfectly appropriate to taste before you buy. Some bakeries have certain days when certain flavors of cake are offered as samples. Find out and taste! If you and your fiancé can't agree on a flavor of cake, filling, or frosting, ask your pastry chef to vary the fillings from layer to layer, giving each of you your favorite flavors.

Though some pastry chefs disagree, your choice of wedding cakes often seems to be either extraordinarily delicate decorations or good flavor. A cake can either taste terrific and look pretty good, or it can look like Valentine lace and taste like cardboard be-

> **HOW WE DID IT**
> Tom just didn't like wedding cake. Instead, we had miniature chocolate cream tarts made and displayed them on glass tiered cake plates, so they looked like a wedding cake. We put our wedding cake topper on the top tier.
> —*Shelly and Tom, 35 and 46*

cause certain types of decorating are best done on dry (even frozen) cakes. You probably won't eat much of the cake anyway, so if the look is what's important to you, choose your bakery accordingly.

If you want a delicious cake and wish its decorations were more stunning, augment the frosting with fresh flowers on the tiers. Order these flowers from your florist and have your florist arrange them on the cake, or ask the baker to arrange them when your cake is assembled. Let your caterer know which arrangement you choose, so he or she can oversee that detail.

❧ WEDDING CUSTOM HISTORY ❧

The custom of feeding each other wedding cake has its origins in early Roman days, when a bread bun was broken over the head of the bride as a fertility symbol. In the middle ages, couples kissed over a pile of buns.

How much cake do you need?

Wedding cake bakers usually plan on servings the size of a pack of playing cards. If you'd like to serve your guests real dessert-sized slices of cake, tell your baker, so the size of your cake may be planned accordingly. Talk over serving sizes with your caterer, so the cake slices will be cut to your specifications.

❧ TIP ❧

If you wish, you can freeze the top layer of your cake and eat it on your first anniversary. It's a romantic idea, but don't

Liquor

What type of liquor you choose to serve—or whether you choose to serve any—is up to you and your fiancé. There may be strong customs in your community, but the choice is still yours to make. Options include these:

- Serving champagne after your receiving line

- Serving champagne for your toasts

- Serving wine with dinner

- An open bar, hosted by you, open for the entire reception

- An open bar, hosted by you, open only after dinner or during your dance

One way to control alcohol consumption is to serve wine and/or liquor at each table, rather than have an open bar where guests can order. However, doing so can delay service to the guests. A frank discussion with your caterer about your concerns ("We don't want drunk guests!") can help you find a solution that's right for you.

❧ Etiquette Note ❧

Unless your community's custom is different, providing a cash bar (asking guests to pay for their drinks) is considered bad manners. It's better to limit the hours of liquor service or the types of liquor to fit your budget and your concerns.

Setting Up the Reception

Your caterer, your reception-site coordinator, or someone else of your choosing should be handling the wedding day reception details for you, so all you have to do is arrive and have fun. Everything from the first toast to dinner to serving the cake requires your presence, so if you have to check personally on the menu or decorating details, everything will be delayed. Appoint someone to be in charge of managing preparations for the reception.

Set the Order of Reception Events

You and your new husband have the ceremony behind you and all your best friends and loved ones with you. On with the party! Think through the order of events from the point of view of you and your wedding party, from the point of view of your children, and from the point of view of your guests. Ideally, you'll want to keep your guests comfortable, keep things moving, prevent any unnecessary waits for your children and your guests, and allow you and your groom to enjoy your family and guests.

❖ TIP ❖

Tell the members of your wedding party that you'll be waiting for them, so you can start the receiving line (just in case someone decides to stop for fast food along the way).

Getting to the reception

Plan for your transportation from the ceremony to the reception site. If possible, bring your children in the limo or car with you—they'll enjoy the fun. Don't forget to plan transportation for your children, your parents, and your wedding party. You'll need everyone there at once, so you can start the receiving line.

Decide how traffic will flow best from one site to another. If you don't want to travel from the ceremony site to the reception site, consider getting married in a hotel, hall, bed-and-breakfast, or other site where your wedding can smoothly and instantly transition into your reception. If you are getting married in a church or temple or have chosen a site that can't accommodate a reception, you'll need to decide how best to direct guests from one place to the other. How will the traffic logically flow? How should ushers direct guests to leave the church or temple? Don't forget to include in your invitation a map with directions for guests from the church or temple to the reception site.

> **HOW WE DID IT**
> Because we felt our reception was about our friends and family, we decorated each table with a cluster of framed photographs of the people we invited to sit at that table. These were wonderful conversation starters and helped us let all the guests know how important they are in our lives.
> —*Cissy, 39*

Plan a logical flow of guest traffic

Plan with your site coordinator or caterer for the smoothest flow of traffic possible. If the weather requires outerwear (or even raincoats and umbrellas), plan for a coat-check room (with or without a staff person taking coats). If you're having a home reception, buy several inexpensive rolling laundry carts and stock them with hangers, or rent coat racks. Designate one bedroom or other room as the "coat room" and ask a family member, friend, or member of the catering staff to direct arrivals there.

Set up your receiving line near (but not blocking) the entrance. If your guest list is small, you can probably get by with just providing coffee or champagne until everyone has been through the receiving line. If your guest list is large and the receiving line may take some time, consider offering light appetizers to your guests. It is not appropriate for your guests to begin eating the main meal until you and your new husband are seated.

Your receiving line

A receiving line allows you, your groom, your parents, and your wedding party to greet and speak briefly with each guest. Depending on the size of your wedding and the schedule of events, these may be the only moments you'll spend more-or-less privately with guests. It's a lovely courtesy to extend to them, and it's just good manners.

Some couples choose to have their receiving line form in the back of the church and then greet guests as they leave for the reception. If this is the custom in your community, fine. There are good reasons to wait and hold the receiving line at your reception, however. Having it in the church backs up traffic, making guests wait in their pews for some time. If there is a wedding right after yours, guests for the next wedding could be arriving while your guests are still trying to leave. The first guests through your receiving line will arrive at your reception long before you, and all your guests will get to the reception before you. The earliest arrivals will have to wait for some time without food (although you could arrange to have drinks served before you arrive).

If possible, hold your receiving line at your reception site. The guests will arrive and be greeted by someone who can direct them to the coat check and then to the receiving line. When the guests leave the receiving line, they can sip champagne, have appetizers (if you're serving them), visit with other guests, or sit at their tables. The moment the last guest moves through the line, you can start the champagne toasts and serve your refreshments.

If your ceremony and reception are at the same site, work with your site coordinator and/or caterer to work out a logical traffic-flow pattern.

Who's in your receiving line?

The receiving line is for hosts to greet their guests and for guests to get to greet and meet the newlyweds and their parents. Strict formal rules state that the receiving line is for hosts only, which means that if your parents are divorced and only Mom is paying for your wedding, Dad has no business standing in line. This ought to irritate Dad and create quite a bit of family friction that will last into perpetuity. If your parents are divorced and you wish to be utterly proper, if your mother gives your reception, she stands in your receiving line and your father, a guest, does not. If your mother has a new husband, he doesn't stand there either; he just mills around somewhere trying to not get into a fight with your father. If your father hosts the reception, he gets to stand in line. If he hasn't remarried, your mother may stand with him. If he has remarried, your mother does not stand with him. His wife does not stand in the line. I have no patience for any of this nonsense and vote for creating a receiving line out of all the people who have loved and raised you.

WHO STANDS WHERE?
A typical receiving line order:

1. Bride's mother and father
2. Groom's mother and father
3. Bride
4. Groom
5. Bride's maid of honor
6. Bride's attendants (Optional. I don't know why grooms-men aren't expected to talk and make nice with the guests, but traditionally, they aren't.)

A commonsense option:

1. Bride and groom (At your age, you two know your guests better than your parents do—you'll put your parents at ease by introducing your guests to them.)
2. Bride's mother and father (or stepfather)
3. Groom's mother and father (or stepfather)
4. Bride's father and stepmother
5. Groom's father and stepmother
6. Bride's maid of honor
7. Bride's attendants (optional)

A nice touch is to have a waiter bring trays of champagne to guests who are waiting to go through the line (if it is long) or bring them to guests as they exit the line.

Children in the receiving line

If your children are in your wedding party, they may certainly be in your receiving line. If your children are young, however, be realistic. Your children can participate; just be prepared for them to come and go as their interest waxes and wanes. Have the baby-sitter ready to take them out of the line and entertain them until you and your groom join the reception. If you'd like your older children with you in the receiving line, then have them there.

Bride's table

This table is often a long, narrow table (think Leonardo Da Vinci's *Last Supper*) facing your guests, so all your guests can see you during dinner and for toasts. Traditionally, you and your husband sit in the center, with his best man on your right, your maid of honor on his left, and the rest of your wedding party and their spouses in the remaining seats. The less formal atmosphere of second weddings allows you some leeway. If your wedding party is small, include your parents and/or your children. Another good option is a special children's table, placed near yours.

With a buffet, you and your husband, your wedding party, your parents, and your children should be the first in line. To avoid juggling a plate and serving yourself, consider having the catering staff fill plates and bring them to the bride's table. Once you and your table are seated and eating, the rest of the guests can begin.

With a sit-down dinner, you and your husband, your wedding party, your parents, and your children should sit at the bride's table. The guests will take this cue and take their own seats. Then dinner can be served.

Place cards

You may wish to write out a place card for each guest and set up seating arrangements. Finding a card with your name on it and a place waiting for you can be a welcoming, gracious feeling for a guest. (It can also be great fun for children! Decorate their cards with sequins, foil stars, and ribbons.) Place cards spare guests that awkward moment of standing around, wondering where to sit. When you make seating arrangements, mix up your friends and your fiancé's friends, your family and his family, while grouping people with similar interests to encourage lively conversation. (Don't worry too much about starting conversations—everyone can talk about your lovely wedding!)

Toasts

Traditionally, the best man offers the first toast to the couple, just before the cake is cut. Another good time for toasts is after everyone is seated and before dinner is served. The groom, the fathers, and the stepfathers may also offer toasts, and depending on the formality of your wedding, special friends may do so as well. If your children are older, one or all of them may offer a toast.

Do ask "toasters" not to go on and on about your marital history and past spouses. While you and your spouse may be able to laugh at a mild joke, other guests may have hurt feelings—your children and your family members, for instance. This isn't the place or the time.

Displaying Gifts

In some communities, it is customary to display your gifts at the reception, especially if the reception is at home. If your reception is not held at home, you need not transport gifts given to you before your wedding to your reception site to display them on your wedding day. And, as a second-time bride, following this custom is optional, even if it is expected of first-time brides.

If you do display gifts, don't display checks or cash gifts. If you have duplicate gifts, don't display them near each other. Try to group gifts in thoughtful ways—don't put a modest gift next to an extravagant one.

Some couples ask a friend to open gifts and display them at the reception. Others open gifts themselves the morning after the wedding. Sometimes they do so with close friends and family present, perhaps at a day-after brunch. Assign someone to keep a clear, written record of who gave which gift, so you can send thank-you notes later.

❧ Etiquette Note ❧

Do not take time away from your reception guests to stop and open gifts yourselves.

Reception Music

What you select for reception music will depend on the time of day of your reception and on whether or not you have dancing. A reception at any time of day benefits from soft, background music from a harp, classical guitar, piano, or small string ensemble. If your reception includes dinner, similar background music is appropriate. If you can't afford a band to play during dinner and are saving it for the dancing, then CDs or tapes are appropriate.

It is considered more formal to have a live band, but if you can only afford a DJ, it doesn't mean that your wedding must be a barn dance. Ask the DJ to play music that suits the mood of your reception. If you want a rollicking sock hop, your DJ will oblige. If you want Ella Fitzgerald and Frank Sinatra, the DJ can do that, too. Talk with the DJ about whether you want him or her to act as an emcee. Some couples want a lively, joking DJ; others want music and no talking. Work it out before your wedding—or send your father over to ask the DJ to pipe down.

❧ Etiquette Note ❧

If you're playing CDs or tapes for background music, don't dash in and out from talking to guests to change the tapes. It's best to prerecord tapes from various CDs, number them in the order you want them played, and then designate a person on the reception staff to change the tapes as needed. Playing tapes over the site's speaker system is more tasteful and looks less tacky than having a tape player sitting in the corner.

Dancing

The bride and groom dance first, to a song you two have chosen. This may be "your song," but if your song is "Jeremiah Was a Bullfrog," you may wish to choose something with a little more decorum.

Your parents and your children may join you on the dance floor for the second dance. The band or you and your husband may cue them, or they may just begin dancing. First, you dance with your father and your husband with your mother; then you with your father-in-law and your husband with his mother.

Another dance sequence: The bride and groom, then the bride with her father and the groom with the bride's mother, then the bride's father with the groom's mother and bride's mother with the groom's father, then the ushers with the bridesmaids.

Or, in real life, your 4-year-old may just run out on the dance floor and grab you around the legs, signaling that everyone should start dancing.

❧ ETIQUETTE NOTE ❦

If you have divorced parents who have remarried, and it boggles your mind to invent a dance sequence that does not alienate any of them, skip it entirely. Dance your first dance with your new husband and then be sure that you each dance with all your parents and stepparents within the first few dances.

Young Children at Your Reception

Think like a child for a moment. How fun does this sound? Dress up in stiff, scratchy clothes. Try to sit still during a boring church ceremony. Put up with everybody else fussing over Mom, who barely has time for you. Try to sit still during a boring reception. Act happy when Mom leaves for two weeks and you have to stay with yukky old Aunt Mildred.

You and your fiancé will have a much more romantic, enjoyable wedding if you build in some kid-friendly atmosphere that's appropriate to the ages of your children.

❧ KIDS TALK ❧

My favorite part of the wedding was the chocolate sundae.
—*Brittany, 5*

TIPS FOR A KID-FRIENDLY RECEPTION

❧ Give them their own table, set with fun activities and a snack they can eat immediately to avoid the hungry grumpies.

❧ Set the children's table differently from the other guests' tables: no breakable centerpiece, no fussy napkins, no china and crystal. Choose sturdy tableware you won't worry about and add fun details: balloons, wrapped gifts for each child, and games.

◆ Don't set the children's table with party favors or other items that can become projectiles, weapons, and paper airplanes.

◆ Serve the children first, so they don't get cranky.

◆ Have your children help you plan their own reception menu and include their favorite foods.

◆ Hire a magician to do tricks; a storyteller to read; or a clown to entertain them, do face painting, make balloon animals, and do other fun things.

◆ Hire their favorite babysitter to sit at their table with them and supervise.

Older Children at Your Reception

Grown children obviously don't need a baby-sitter or a special menu, but they do need to feel important to you. Don't treat your children and new step-children just like other guests. Give them flowers to carry or wear. Seat them in places of honor at your table or a table near you. Introduce them during the toasts. Thank them for their support. And be aware of their own special sensitivities at this time—of course, they'll be thinking of their mom or dad who isn't there. Understand that, for them, this event may be tinged with feelings of uneasiness or even grief. If whatever you say seems not quite right, remember that an understanding look and a loving hug speak volumes.

> **HOW WE DID IT**
> We had a second wedding cake that the children decorated, not with a little plastic bride and groom, but with toys and dolls that symbolized their own hobbies and talents: football and hockey guys, a trumpet-playing Smurf, a Star Trek action figure.
> —*Bill, 40*

Watch What You Say

A friend recently remarried years after his first wife died of cancer. At the reception, which his grown sons attended, the groom made a lengthy speech about how he had *never* been so happy and that this was *the* happiest day of his life. Though his sons liked his new bride, they both teared up at the thought that their parents' wedding and their own births hadn't made their father this happy. Of course, that wasn't what their dad meant, but the damage was done. Think like a child before you speak.

Wedding Favors

It may be the custom in your community to give wedding favors to your guests. Or you may just like the idea and want to adopt it. A favor may be set at each guest's place at a sit-down dinner or handed to guests by a friend or young child as they leave (arrange the favors prettily in a basket or display). Your budget and creativity are your only limits here. If your wedding has a theme, choose a favor that fits it. Favors can be wrapped in tissue paper or cellophane and/or simply tied with a ribbon that matches the colors in your wedding.

Ideas for wedding favors:

- ✤ A small box of chocolates

- ✤ A gourmet truffle, wrapped in cellophane and tied with a ribbon

- ✤ Almonds, wrapped in white netting and tied with a ribbon

- ✤ A small piece of crystal or a porcelain figurine

- ✤ A holiday ornament

- ✤ A napkin ring

Traditions, and How to
Avoid Them

You may love the wedding reception traditions of tossing the garter and throwing the bouquet. If so, indulge! But if you feel these activities are not appropriate or desirable, don't have them. No problem.

Removing and tossing the garter

Some brides hike up their skirts, plant their high heel on a chair, and let their groom remove the garter with his teeth. You can be more discreet, if you like, turning your back on the crowd and asking your husband to behave with a bit more decorum. Traditionally, he then tosses your garter to his ushers and single men from your wedding party. If you don't have many single men, any guys will do.

❧ WEDDING CUSTOM HISTORY ❧

According to some accounts, the groom removing and tossing the bride's garter to a crowd of men has its origins in the Middle Ages, when wedding guests would tear a bit of lace or fabric off the bride's gown for good luck. Rather than trash her dress and traumatize the bride, this garter custom was developed. Hmm . . .

Throwing your bouquet

If you'd like to keep your bouquet and not throw it away, ask your florist to prepare a smaller nosegay to toss. At my first wedding, I had a small bouquet fashioned inside my larger one, and I simply removed it and tossed it. Traditionally, the bride's bouquet is tossed to all the single women guests. If you don't have many single women guests, the few you do invite may feel singled out, no pun intended.

If you have a daughter or stepdaughter, consider asking her if she'd like to have your bouquet as a keepsake.

Tipping at Your Reception

Your reception site may include gratuities in your bill. But it's a good idea to ask ahead of time and to know if *everyone* who has been helpful to you will share the gratuities.

If gratuities are not included, you'll want to plan ahead. Bring cash and budget for this added expense—it can be a whopper!

You don't want to be handing out cash while you're also trying to be the bride and groom. Give the tips to your best man and ask him to distribute them according to your wishes.

STAFF TO REMEMBER WHEN YOU TIP

✤ Your reception-site consultant or event coordinator. A gratuity for this person may already be written into your reception contract. But if the service has been terrific, an additional tip is always appreciated. About 15–20 percent of your total bill, or a dollar or two per guest, is about right.

- Your caterer. A tip may be included in your bill, but it's often expected that you'll also add something at the time of service. Consider how many waitstaff your caterer has to share your tip with and consider how excellent (or not!) their service was. Again, figure on 15–20 percent of your total catering bill, or just pick a nice, round number.

- Your bartender. If a gratuity is included in your catering or reception bill, figure on another 10–15 percent of your total bar tab as a tip for the bartender.

- Your reception musicians. If you were especially pleased with your DJ or band, tip them. Your DJ contract may include a gratuity. If not, add 15–20 percent of his or her bill to your check. If you're tipping an eight-member band, remember that a $50 tip doesn't go far. If you can afford it, aim for $20–$30 per band member.

- Your coat check and/or greeting staff. If your caterer has provided these people for you, include their tips in your caterer's tip. If your reception site has provided the staff, tip these people separately. A dollar per coat is fine.

- Your parking valet. Have your best man or father pay the valets in advances, so they don't start accepting tips from guests. A tip of a dollar or two per car is standard.

- Your limousine drivers. Before they drive away, tip the drivers who moved you, your family, and your wedding party from home to your wedding and from your wedding to your reception. Again, 15–20 percent of the bill is a good guideline.

Ask your bartender to place a sign on the bar that says, "No tipping, please." Ask your parking valet to have a similar sign at the entrance, and your coat-check person to have a sign at the coat check. These signs tell your guests (and the staff!) that you'll be taking care of the gratuities. Now, don't forget to tip these people!

Leaving for Your Honeymoon

If neither of you have children, you may exit your reception for your honeymoon without a second thought. But if you have children, you'll want to develop a sensitive strategy.

Helping your children adjust

For young children, this is likely to be an exhausting, some-times boring day without much one-on-one time with Mom or Dad. To end it by seeing you drive away in a noisy crowd of people who are throwing things at you is sure to result in a wailing child and a guilty parent. You may wish to leave the dramatic exit from the reception to first-time brides and choose another style for yourself this time around. Options for honeymoon plans are listed in Chapter 11, along with tips on how to help your children deal with your absence.

But no matter what you decide to do about your honey-moon, build in time alone with each child at the end of the reception. Review the plans you've made ("Carl and I will be staying here at the hotel for one night, while you and your sister go stay with Grandma. We'll come pick you up on Sunday."). Reassure your child that you'll be absent for only a certain number of days.

You might try this: Retire from your reception early with your children, and spend a family half-hour reviewing the day's events and talking together before you and your new husband begin your honeymoon.

Every effort you make to reassure, comfort, and include your children now will pay off big as your new, blended family begins its life together. It is wise, wise, wise to devote a little time and thought now to your children's needs—you'll gain it back in spades.

Making your getaway

Though your friends are now old enough to know that trashing a car with shaving cream and old shoes is tacky, you may consider "hiding" the getaway car to avoid such silliness. Ask the best man to be in charge of providing you with this transportation and doing his best to keep the car's whereabouts a secret. He could also help by double checking that there is gas in the vehicle and help the caterer sneak a box meal into the car for you and your husband to eat on the way or later that night. (A surprising number of newlyweds are too busy at their receptions to eat!)

Throwing rice and other hazards

The custom of tossing rice at the departing newlyweds has come under fire. Some guests fire the grain as missiles, catching the bride and groom in the face or eye. Many reception sites discourage the use of rice because it is difficult to clean up. Hard rice is also harmful to some birds and isn't an ecologically sound choice.

- Think about their favorite foods and activities and shop and prepare now for a smooth wedding week later.

- Try to keep your children well rested all week, with naps and bedtimes on regular schedules.

- If your children are older, let them know that it's important for them to be well rested, so they can enjoy your wedding and reception.

- Feed your children before your wedding, pack snacks for emergency use during your wedding, and have something ready for your children to eat and drink immediately following your wedding.

- Plan simple, nutritious snacks—you don't need the children on sugar highs bouncing off the walls.

- Keep your children well hydrated: Make them drink juice and/or water during the hours before your wedding (but not so much that they have a bathroom emergency) and during your reception.

- Hire a baby-sitter whose sole responsibility is to care for your children during your wedding rehearsal, your wedding, and your reception. You can still interact with your children as much as you like, but if your children get fussy at exactly the wrong moment (say, when you are repeating your vows), you'll need a sitter to intervene.

- More than once this week, talk through what to expect on the Big Day. "On Saturday morning, Grandma and Grandpa will be here to help you get ready. There will be a photographer taking pictures, but you don't always have to pose and look nice. There will be a lot of people coming and going, but I'll always be here, and you can always find me. After lunch, Uncle Tom will drive all of us to the church. You'll stay with Aunt Sarah for a while in a room just for you, playing and reading books. Then, she'll bring you into the church, and you'll sit in a special seat, just for you! You'll have your favorite books there to read. You'll have to try and sit still and be extra quiet, but not for very long..."

◆ If your children are older, have a grown-up discussion about their feelings and expectations. If there are rumblings of discontent, a frank talk may be worthwhile. "Look, I know that you have some misgivings about me getting married again. I want you to know that you can always come to me to talk things over. I know we still have some things to work out and that we still need to spend time talking to each other. But I also want to ask you to respect and honor this day. It's important to me. Can we set aside our disagreement about this for a day and just celebrate being a family together?"

Rehearsal

If you think you'll feel more comfortable on your wedding day if you have rehearsed the ceremony beforehand, then schedule a rehearsal. If you feel that your ceremony is straightforward and you feel relaxed, don't rehearse.

If your children are young, at least talk them through what to expect. If possible, bring them to the church or ceremony site beforehand and explain what will be happening.

You may want to ask your site coordinator or wedding consultant to be present at the rehearsal to help direct events.

so that you, your fiancé, and your wedding party can get the timing of your entrances and exits correct.

Your wedding party will practice lining up and entering in order and will learn where they stand during the ceremony.

Readers and speakers will be told when to rise and speak, but they will not perform their readings at the rehearsal.

Your celebrant will talk you through the order of your ceremony, including when to speak your vows and when to exchange rings.

If you wish to practice handing your bouquet to your maid of honor, bring a faux bouquet made of ribbons from one of your showers.

❧ TIP ❧

At your rehearsal, remind your usher to:

- ❧ Ask each guest, "Friend of the bride or groom?" and seat each one accordingly, if that's your wish.

- ❧ Seat guests with reserved pew cards accordingly.

- ❧ Seat your grandparents, parents, and children in order just before the wedding party's entrance (introduce the ushers to these family members now).

Rehearsal Dinner

If you have a wedding rehearsal the night before your wedding, then a rehearsal dinner is expected. If you don't rehearse your ceremony, you may still wish to host a night-before party for your family and out-of-town guests.

Traditionally, the groom's parents host the rehearsal dinner. If they offer to do so, the planning of the dinner is up to them. Furnish them with a list of all the people who should be invited. If the groom's parents live out of town, you may offer to send out invitations in their name.

For a second wedding, your fiancé's parents aren't required to host the event. If they offer, it's gracious. If they don't, go ahead and host the dinner yourselves.

Who pays?

The groom's parents traditionally pay for this dinner. For a second wedding, it's optional for them to pick up the bill. If they don't volunteer, you and your fiancé pay for the dinner.

When is it held?

Immediately after your rehearsal, especially if you have hungry children. Choose a site near your ceremony site, so out-of-town family and friends don't get lost on their way to the restaurant.

Where is it held?

Your rehearsal dinner can be a private room at a favorite restaurant, a catered dinner at a club or hotel, or a dinner in your home (advice: don't cook! You have enough to do!). If your future in-laws are hosting this event, they may hold it at their home.

Whom do you invite?

If you've actually held a wedding rehearsal, it is customary for you to serve a dinner to members of your wedding party, escorts and spouses of members of the wedding party, and the parents of any junior bridesmaids, flower girls, or ring bearers. You should also include your children, whether or not they are in your wedding party, and your siblings. You don't have to invite the celebrant, unless he or she is a family member or good friend.

If you or your fiancé's parents are separated or divorced, you should still invite all the parents. If your parents have remarried, invite their spouses. If your parents are dating others, it may be best not to include the escorts for this event, unless they have serious, long-term relationships. If your parents are all willing to come, but some don't want to sit near each other, set up the event so you can use place cards and position everyone strategically. If one of your parents sticks his or her nose in the air and refuses to attend if "that person" is there, too, try to stay calm. Say something like, "It would really mean a lot to me, Mom, if you'd be there with us, but if you don't feel you can, I understand." Then drop it. Mom may just surprise you and show up. You shouldn't have to think about this silliness at your wedding, but reality is reality.

If you don't want to rehearse your ceremony, this

> **HOW WE DID IT**
> Instead of a rehearsal dinner, we had a party at our house. Things were very relaxed. When our family members or friends arrived from out of town, they just dropped in at the house for a snack and conversation. It was one of our favorite parts of our wedding weekend.
> —*John, 53*

dinner can simply be a gathering of your family, a gathering of your wedding party, or a night-before celebration of friends and family who are in town for the wedding. In this case, invite whomever you please, but certainly include your wedding party, your children, and your families.

Do your children attend?

If your children are in your wedding party, you'll want them present at your rehearsal. If the rehearsal dinner is early enough (if the children are young), they may certainly attend your rehearsal dinner. If the dinner is best suited for adults, you may wish to arrange for a baby-sitter to pick up your children at the rehearsal, take them out for pizza, and bring them home for an early night. Tired children make crabby children at the wedding!

Send rehearsal dinner invitations

Even if your invitations are just handwritten notes, send the written particulars of time, place, and so forth to all members of the wedding party and everyone on your rehearsal dinner invitation list.

Seating arrangements

Making conscious choices about seating arrangements and using place cards can make guests feel welcome and important. The thoughtful placement of family members and members of your wedding party can encourage mixing and help everyone feel more comfortable. If your in-laws are giving this party, determining the seating arrangements is up to them—but you may certainly offer input or even offer to write out the place cards.

The site of your dinner will determine the shape of the table and the outline of your seating arrangements. If you can manage it, seat everyone at one table to encourage conversation and mixing. For a large party, a "U"-shaped table may work best.

The bride and groom are at the center of the table. The best man is on the bride's right, and the maid of honor is on the groom's left. The seating then alternates, boy-girl, from both sides until all members of the wedding party are seated. If your parents or in-laws are hosting, they sit in traditional host positions (the head and foot of the table on the two ends of a "U" table arrangement). If your children are present and they are young, you may wish to set a special table for them with a baby-sitter. If they want to be at the "big table" with the grown-ups, have someone ready to remove them and entertain them if they get restless.

The rehearsal dinner agenda

There's no real business to take care of, but this is a nice time (particularly if the groom's parents are hosting this event) for the groom's father to give a toast. Your father may give a toast of his own. If members of your wedding party wish to toast you, they may. You and/or your fiancé should also toast each other and your parents. A toast to your children would probably be appreciated, too. Most rehearsal dinners are dinners only, saving the dancing for the next night's wedding—and getting wedding party members home early. To look and feel your best, keep this an early-to-bed, low-alcohol affair.

Our wedding was at a hotel, and we dressed in separate rooms. My maid of honor answered the door, and it was room service. My fiancé had called and ordered sandwiches for me and my bridesmaids, so we'd keep our strength up during photos and the ceremony. That was so sweet!

—Marty, 42

The Day of Your Wedding

A few tips to help your wedding day run smoothly:

- Eat something, bride! You don't want to faint at the altar.

- Pack a basket of nutritious, light foods to nibble on while you're doing your makeup and dressing.

- Pack a bridal emergency kit: safety pins, a sewing kit, aspirin, extra pantyhose, hair spray, hand lotion, makeup, tissues, antiperspirant, a toothbrush, and toothpaste.

❧ TIPS ❧

- To smooth over the last few days before your wedding, delegate errands and tasks to family and friends.

- If you remember something you forgot to do, call your caterer or event coordinator and ask him or her to do it for you.

CHAPTER TEN

AVOIDING FASHION FAUX PAS

Darn. Now that you could really *use* a veil to cover those lit-tle laugh lines you earned during your last divorce, it's not exactly de rigueur to wear one the second time because veils are considered to be a sign of virginity.

❧ WEDDING CUSTOM HISTORY ❧

Why do you need "Something old, something new, some-thing borrowed, something blue"?

Something old and *something new* symbolize your two "old" families combining into one new one (especially meaningful to stepfamilies!).

Something borrowed denotes friendliness, a useful value in any marriage.

Something blue represents faithfulness.

Should You Wear White?

Well, how snippy are your friends likely to be? Actually, a white wedding gown started out as a symbol of affluence in Victorian times, became a sign of purity, and has matured into simply the color of celebration and joy.

If your mother rolls her eyes when you inform her of this development and starts to mutter disparaging comments about mutton dressed as lamb, tell her these bits of nuptial history. During the American Revolution, brides wore red as a sign of rebellion (see? Jane Fonda wasn't the first to practice political grandstanding during solemn ceremonies). And during the Civil War, brides wore purple if they were mourning a brother or a father lost in battle. "Something blue" is thought to be a reference to biblical days, when brides wore a band of blue around the bottom of their wedding costumes to symbolize fidelity and love.

Where, one wonders, are the wedding costume rituals and customs for men? Where are the symbols of men's fidelity, love, affluence, and virginity? Perhaps grooms should wear brown, as a sign that they will cook three times a week and do dishes on off-nights. Carry something pink to signify their support for women's rights. Part their hair on the left to symbolize their willingness to use politically correct pronouns. Use a tie tack as a signal of their promise to stop and ask for directions when lost on a car trip.

But I digress. We were searching through your closet, not his.

Bring a Friend

If you try something on and the heavens open up and the angels sing, that's a sign—it's meant to be your wedding dress, and you should buy it. To know if this is happening, you need to bring along your best friend in the world—the one who will tell you when your rear looks too big, your chest looks too small, and your skin just went so sallow you look like you need jaundice treatments.

When I shopped for my third wedding dress, I brought along my husband. This was a bad plan. The lad was so sweet and agreeable, he told me I looked beautiful in everything. Whatever I wore out of the dressing room caused his eyes to mist over and sent him scrambling for a handkerchief. I ordered a deep green cocktail dress from a famous British designer, plopped down a sizable check, and waited for the dress to arrive. It came late—two days before the wedding. There was no time for a seamstress, so I took the box over to my mother's, and she got out her sewing box. When I emerged from the bathroom wearing this emerald creation, her face fell. "Well," she said, tactfully, "if you had purposely tried to find something to make you look shorter and fatter, you couldn't have done any better." Needless to say, I didn't wear that dress.

But I advise against shopping with mothers, in general, because they easily revert to those years when they decided what you should wear and because they grew up trying to dress like June Cleaver. Instead, I recommend shopping with an honest best friend.

Before you head out for the stores, pick up a passel of bridal fashion magazines. But be prepared. If you think purchasing feminine products in public is embarrassing, wait until you try buying bride magazines accompanied by your six-foot teenage son. Ask your fiancé to buy them for you and deliver them to you secretly, wrapped in brown paper for you to pore over behind locked doors. So what if you're 35, carry a bulging briefcase, and understand how adjustable rate mortgages work? You're still a girl, and you're having a wedding. Go ahead and act like an engaged person.

❧ Don't Forget! ❧

Do you have:

- a garter to toss?
- a pretty linen handkerchief to cry into?
- jewelry: necklace, earrings, bracelet?
- hair accessories?

What Style Can I Wear the Second Time Around?

Bottom line: You can wear whatever you want to wear, honey.

Most of the world thinks that hoop-skirted, bead-covered bright white gowns with fourteen-foot trains and yards of netting on the veil are for first-time brides only. Even so, that still leaves you lots of other choices. There are tons of options that lie between teen-bride rhinestones and matronly, mother-of-the-bride formals.

Even conservative etiquette manuals now state that white suits and gowns are perfectly acceptable bridal wear for the encore bride. Though white was once considered to be a color signifying virginity, it is now thought of as simply a symbol of celebration: so wear white if you like, solo or accessorized with color.

Blusher veils are supposed to symbolize virginity, so they should not be worn for a second wedding unless your religious custom always includes a veil. But remember Ivana Trump (a lovely woman, but certainly not made of driven snow with her daughter as a bridesmaid) and her odd veil when she remarried after Donald? *Psst*—don't trim your veil in thick ribbon like Ivana; she looked bisected. But she wanted a veil, so she wore one. If you want one, drape it around a wonderful hat (it takes a grown woman to wear a hat properly). Hats with veils, flowers, and combs are acceptable hairpieces for second brides.

Lengthy trains are typically for first-time brides. However, evening gowns and ballgowns often have a slight "fishtail" hemline extension in the back—such a modest train is fine.

So now that you know the rules, be like Picasso. Once he mastered traditional painting techniques, he threw all the rules out the window and did his own thing. You're a mature woman now. You have your own style. Do what you want.

The advantage you have over a first-time bride is that you have been dressing your body for more than twenty-one years. You have dressed for a variety of social gatherings and formal events. You know what flatters you and what doesn't. And you've already dressed yourself once in a bridal costume. You remember what felt good about it and what didn't. Did you always wish you had worn a train? Hated those short sleeves you settled for? Wished the skirt was narrower, wider, longer, fuller, slit a little higher? Get what you want this time. Now's your chance to use all your feminine experience and dress yourself to dazzle, in your own inimitable style.

If *you* feel you are "too old" for a wedding dress and won't look your best in one, try

- A stunning designer cocktail dress

- An elegant evening gown

- Anything cream- or gold-colored (it'll flatter your complexion)

- A gorgeous evening suit

✦ WEDDING CUSTOM HISTORY ✦

The bride's father places a penny in the bride's shoe to encourage prosperity in the marriage. Tradition doesn't say whether it's the bride's or the groom's prosperity that's supposed to grow.

If You're Shopping for a Real Bridal Gown

Rip out all the pictures of dresses with bits of your favorite stuff: the best sleeves, most flattering neckline, your favorite fabric, and so forth. Take these pictures along when you shop, but don't be surprised if no store can find these exact dresses for you. Many dresses that are shown in bridal ads are never "cut"—only one dress is made for the photo session, and you won't find copies on a rack anywhere. But you can try on dresses with those kinds of features and perhaps find something you like. And if you can't find anything at a store, you can show your portfolio to a seamstress and have a design custom made.

Visit a full-service bridal salon

If you shop at discount bridal shops, try to avoid the ones that offer little or no service. The few dollars you may save you'll more than pay for in aggravation and inconvenience. During the coming weeks, you will probably be juggling a thousand wedding details, plus a job and children, and you will appreciate the service a high-quality salon can provide. And a young bride may be able to get away with wearing a gown sewn of cheaper material that is inexpertly cut. But an older (even slightly older) bride can't carry such a gown off without looking tacky. You want to look confident and elegant. You want the shopping to be nearly as fun as the wedding. If you're on a tight budget, even full-service salons are likely to have some dresses in your price range. Stick with legitimate salons with clearance or marked-down first-quality dresses. Another option: Some salons offer dresses for rent, an increasingly popular option that may be offered near you. Ask area salons if they rent gowns or know who does.

Make an appointment

After you've found the best few bridal salons in your area, phone each of them. At most salons, you can't just walk in off the street—you need to have an appointment. When you call, be prepared to tell the salon receptionist how formal your wedding will be, that you are a second-time bride, and what price range you are considering for your dress. The receptionist may also ask if you want a train or no train on your dress (trains are usually reserved for the first-time, big church wedding, but don't automatically rule them out—some trains are only a brief bit of hem trailing behind, which can look quite

At my first wedding, I wore an ivory gown with a huge veil and long train that I bought on sale at a department store for $68. I hated it, but I could afford it. At my second wedding, I wore a gorgeous cocktail dress of heavy coral silk, trimmed at the cuffs with glass beads. I still wear it now and then. For my third wedding, I bought an off-the-rack midnight blue velvet dress by Kathryn Conover that was trimmed in satin, hand-rolled roses. I wore that a few times again, too. This last time, with a maid-of-honor daughter the age I was at my first wedding, I bought a really-for-truly wedding gown of faintly beige silk shantung, cut more like a ball gown than a bridal gown, with no headpiece, tons of skirt, and a low neckline. "You and your breasts," said my friend, Cate, in the reception line, "are lovely." Of all my wedding dresses, that one is my favorite. Why? Because it reflected exactly how I felt then and still do—shamelessly romantic; lucky as a princess; and much more confident, happy, and in love than any 18-year-old could ever be.

elegant and is acceptable for encore brides). All these details will help the staff make a selection for you.

Ask for a consultant who is older than 18 (this is crucial) and has some experience dressing "mature" or encore brides. The consultant may ask you to tell her what kind of dress you want ahead of time. You're old enough to know what you look good in and what doesn't flatter you, so tell your her what to choose and what to discard. If you truly don't know the style of formal gown that would look best on you, if you are still trying to decide the degree of formality of your wedding, or if you just want to try on a lot of dresses, ask the consultant to pull a broad selection of styles.

Wear clean underwear

Before your shopping day, buy a strapless long-line bra or bustier in white and a pair of decent panties that cover your stretch marks. Strangers will be staring at you in your underwear, so it should be clean, help you look your best under a dress, and cover the parts you want covered. Don't buy a strapless, one-piece teddy—a separate bustier gives you more lift and support, and the one-piece numbers tend to inch ever downward slowly and inexorably, causing you to tug at your bodice all day (and on your wedding day, all through your reception). It's a fashion faux pas, and it looks bad in photos. A strapless bustier will give you a flattering waistline and smooth bodice, and it will show off formal gowns with illusion netting and/or open necklines to their best advantage.

Remember to bring along pantyhose and a pair of dress shoes with heels at your favorite height. Toss everything in a bag. This stuff is for trying-on-times only. Wear comfortable shoes and clothes while you travel from shop to shop.

Eat sensibly

Then, take your magazine clips, your bag of stuff, and your best friend and go out for breakfast. Shopping for a wedding dress is almost, but not quite, in the daunting category of shopping for a bathing suit. You may be tempted to skip eating to squeeze into a smaller size, but don't—you need to eat well enough to keep your energy and mood level up. If your blood sugar crashes, you'll get crabby and imagine that you look dreadful in everything. Eat light foods if you wish, but be sure to have some protein. Afterward, if you succeed, treat yourselves to a hot fudge sundae.

This is not really a lighthearted suggestion. Your wedding gown is likely to represent a significant financial investment. It will probably be the most expensive dress you ever buy. Don't forget, the dresses of your attendants and the degree of formality of your entire wedding and reception will follow your wardrobe choice. So stay focused, take good care of yourself, and help yourself make the best decision you can make.

❧ TIP ❧

Ask your bridal salon consultant how you should care for your dress after you bring it home. Should it be unzipped from its bag? Should you remove the tissue stuffing or leave it in?

A good bridal salon will have a large dressing room, plus a Diet Coke and a chair for your friend. Your friend can hold the folder of torn-out pictures of dresses you like and play bad cop to your good cop. When you start to cave in to what the consultant likes best, your friend (whose legs won't hurt as much and who will have the

advantage of having had a caffeine boost) will remind you of everything you told her to remind you of in the car on the way to the salon.

Even if you are sure you don't want to wear a wedding gown, don't rule out bridal salons. There are many of us encore brides out there, and salons now offer pastel gowns, cocktail dresses, and other options for second weddings. Many wedding gowns are available in white and off-white, and some are even available in beige, taupe, and light pastel shades. Bridal salons are also accustomed to fitting brides-maids and (sorry to say this) mothers of the bride and can offer you a selection of evening gowns. A bridal salon will have the best selection of cuts, styles, fabrics, and colors in dresses that fall into the ballgown/cocktail party/wedding/coronation category.

Add alterations and tailoring

If you find a nearly perfect dress that is missing one or two details, ask the consultant if she can have them added for you. Often, dresses can be cut shorter or made longer, have trains added or removed, have a row of fabric-covered buttons sewn up the back, and have sleeves removed or added.

Shop early

Many bridal gowns take six months to order, so start shopping early. More and more bridal shops are also stocking off-the-rack dresses you can buy and take home the same day, or buy and have altered in a few weeks. You can also rent a bridal gown, if you wish, but these gowns still need to be reserved well in advance. If you want to wear an evening gown, special occasion dress, or designer gown, you should still shop early to allow for alterations and special orders. Plus, decisions about what your wedding party, children, mother and mother-in-law will wear hinge on your own dress choice. So start shopping as soon as you can.

Make a deposit and get a date

If you find the perfect gown (hooray!), you'll be asked to pay a deposit—probably about half the cost of the dress—when you order. Ask if you can get a guaranteed delivery date and set it several days or even weeks before your actual wedding date. A wedding dress that arrives during your honeymoon is useless.

❧ TIP ❧

When you shop for everyday and work clothes, you probably don't think of using alterations to omit or add sleeves, add a row of buttons, or make other sweeping changes to a dress.

But at a bridal salon, such changes are commonplace. Alter an existing dress to suit your own style. If a gown is too bare, add illusion net or cap sleeves. If you love a sleeveless gown but want to cover your upper arms, have invisible fasteners sewn into an elegant bridal shawl to hold it in picturesque place, softly draping your shoulders.

No Wedding Gown, Please

If a wedding gown is not for you, a second wedding is a great excuse to pick up a stunning little something that can later be worn to the symphony, out to dinners, or on your anniversary. Here's your chance to treat yourself to an evening gown, cocktail dress, or top-of-the-line designer suit that you truly *can* wear again. And don't overlook shopping at bridal shops—remember that they also stock tea-length gowns, elegant wedding suits, cocktail dresses, and formal gowns.

Indulge and have your dress altered to fit you perfectly. You'll look wonderful.

❦ TIP ❦

Don't forget the internet! A growing number of salons, gown designers, and wedding registries are going online. Key in "weddings" or "wedding AND gowns" or "wedding AND registry."

Starting from Scratch

If you can't find the perfect dress at a shop, consider having one made for you. Look for a custom designer of formal wear in your area. Increasingly, seamstresses are specializing in second-wedding bridal wear. Check the yellow pages.

It is also completely appropriate for a second-time bride to wear her mother's or grandmother's wedding dress. You'll want to have the dress altered to fit you, and you may wish to replace a veil with a hat or simple flowers. If you feel that white is too "first time" for you, add a colored sash or accent.

❧ ETIQUETTE NOTE ❧

It is not appropriate to wear your old wedding gown or anything you wore at a previous wedding. Your wardrobe for this wedding should be new to you, even if some of the pieces are vintage.

❧ TIP ❧

Ask your bridal salon, dressmaker, or tailor to add underarm shields to your gown. These shields can be removed and are disposable, but provide terrific protection during an excitement-filled day. And they can help you relax, knowing you'll look your best for photographs.

Budget Stretchers

Wedding gowns, evening gowns, cocktail dresses, and dressy suits are all available in a variety of price ranges. Other cost-saving ideas: Look for sales on ready-to-wear gowns, buy a floor sample, or rent a gown (even evening gowns can be rented). Don't forget to ask if alterations are included in the price of your gown.

The Rest of Your Wardrobe

At the bridal salon, settle on the best heel height for your dress. Take a swatch of fabric from your dress (you'll need it to choose shoes, accessories, wedding party dresses, and more). Buy a pair of shoes for photos and your wedding and consider buying a more comfortable pair for dancing at your reception.

You'll need a small evening bag for touchups throughout the day. Equip it with a mirror, lipstick, handkerchief, comb, and compact.

With all the time you'll spend on your feet on your wedding day, support hose is a good idea. Buy several pair and bring them with you in your wedding emergency kit, in case of runs or snags.

No, you do not need to wear a garter or remove it to stripper music and toss it to your ushers during the reception. Your call.

You'll think I'm kidding, but an utterly proper-looking bridal consultant gave me this suggestion, so I'll pass it along. If you choose a gown with a large, full skirt and crinolines, consider wearing crotchless pantyhose or a garter belt and stockings with crotchless panties or with no panties at all. No, I'm not being obscene. Here's why: Going to the bathroom becomes a thorny problem when you're dealing with lots of skirt and a train. You may need an attendant on either side of you holding up your skirts. If you're on your own, holding your skirt up with one hand and sliding your pantyhose down with the other is nearly impossible.

What Can My Wedding Party Wear?

Something that suits what you're wearing—and, if you're feeling particularly gracious, also flatters them.

A small wedding party

If your wedding party is small, say, just a maid of honor and a best man, you may go shopping with your maid of honor and pick something off the rack. If you trust her taste, simply ask her to choose her own dress within a certain color and style range. If you need to coordinate styles and colors with your dress, perhaps a flower girl's, a junior bridesmaid's, or your daughter's, then you should do the choosing.

Several bridesmaids

If you have several bridesmaids and some live out of town, send them the phone number of your dress shop and have your bridesmaids phone in their measurements. If you have to do so, be sure to have their dresses delivered to them extra early to allow time for alterations. Remember to take swatches from the dresses to dye the shoes—and dye all the shoes at once in one dye lot. Help your busy bridesmaids out by choosing coordinating pantyhose, nail polish, and lipstick and delivering a "bridesmaid package" to each. If you want their jewelry to match, you may buy them earrings or necklaces as a gift.

Flower girl and ring bearer

Your flower girl, if you have one, may carry a basket filled with real or paper-flower petals, which she can scatter on the aisle runner. Or she may simply carry a charming basket of flowers.

If you have a ring bearer, he may wear a dress suit in white or in a color that coordinates with your attendants' dresses. He may also wear a miniature tuxedo, if the groom, best man, and ushers are wearing tuxedoes. Your ring bearer carries a pillow with ribbons sewn on it that tie through your rings and keep them from falling off. If you prefer, you can tie play rings on the pillow and let your best man and matron of honor keep the real rings for you.

Typically, members of the wedding party pay for their own dresses and tuxedoes (or suits).

If you feel that lookalike bridesmaids aren't right for your ceremony, consider picking one color and letting your bridesmaids choose their own styles.

Dressing Your Children: Do I Have to Wear a Suit?

Surprise! Your idea of sartorial splendor and that of your 8-year-old son don't match. You'd like to see him in a miniature Brooks Brothers suit with an old school tie and polished wingtips, and he thinks clean sneakers will be spiffy enough. Another surprise! Shopping with your teenage daughter is not a fun mother-daughter outing; it's a day spent listening to "Gross! That dress is so *ugly!*" over and over and over and over.

❧ DO ❧

Make clothes hunting with the children into a fun event. Give each child his or her own day with you to shop and don't bring your fiancé along.

Use psychology

You can try several tactics. One is the peas versus carrots tactic, which I must credit to my mother. She always said, "Don't give a child a choice between eating vegetables and not eating vegetables. Give him a choice between eating peas or eating carrots." Don't offer to let your children wear whatever they want. *You* pick two or three ensembles as the semifinalists and let your children do the final choosing. Give your children power, but don't give yourself a migraine.

Try to join forces

Another tactic is to look through magazines with your children and find pictures of how they want to look. Find out what cool looks like to them. See if you can live with it. Have your negotiating conversations at home, on the couch, where pouting is less of a public spectacle. It also saves you a certain amount of wandering through stores asking, "Do you like this? Do you like this?" and getting nothing but a stony glare for an answer.

Even if your teen sports a shaved head and pierced body parts, it's appropriate to honor a big event by showering, clipping one's nails, and sprucing up a little around the edges. Don't embarrass your children by insulting their taste ("You're not wearing *those*, are you?") but do help educate them for life ("This is the sort of event people typically dress up for. Now, how would you like to look?").

❧ KIDS TALK ❧

I absolutely did *not* want to wear a suit. My dad said I could wear a sweater and a tie. I was pretty handsome, even when I took off the tie to dance.

—*Michael, 9*

If you're living with rebels

Your children and stepchildren-to-be may choose to rebel against your marriage by making an angry fashion statement. If the rebellion is aimed at you, call in the troops and ask a favorite aunt or uncle (who is, no doubt, *way* cooler than you) to take the little darling shopping. If this tactic works, your child may be convinced to dress a few degrees to the right of obnoxiously. Or, buy a reasonably hip yet appropriate outfit and just hang it in your child's closet. No argument, no big deal. It's simply there. Chances are, come the wedding day, the Rebel Without Any Clothes will feel silly wearing jeans and Birkenstocks while the entire family is dressed to kill. He or she won't want to say "Gee, Mom, you were right," but if there is an appropriate choice available, pressed, and ready, it just may get worn. Don't panic. Unless the wedding is tomorrow, it's likely the rebel will calm down before your big day.

The worst-case scenario: Your teen shows up in clothes that scream "I'm trying to piss you off!" Here's what you do: Tell her you love her and go have your wedding. Clothes are only clothes, but your children are your heart and soul. Your child will remember forever that you welcomed and loved her even when she embarrassed you on purpose. That's a big message.

❧ KIDS TALK ❧

My daughter, Gretchen, wrote in my fourth wedding guest book: "Dear Mom, I promise not to be a jerk this time."

Import a third party as fashion police

The day of my fourth wedding, I hired the stylist from our favorite salon to spend the afternoon in our hotel room, "doing" the hair of my children and a few visiting cousins. It kept them all giggling, happy, and occupied, and we didn't have to argue with anyone about using too much mousse or not having a straight part. Whatever the stylist said was golden, and the children followed her advice without argument.

❧ KIDS TALK ❧

Kids hate loafers, but Mom said sneakers would look stupid, so I had to wear loafers. She let me wear sneakers to breakfast the next day.

—*Brian, 10*

What Do Your Parents Wear?

Your mother chooses her dress, then calls your future mother-in-law to say, "I chose a street-length blue suit." Then your mother-in-law can go shopping to find something that will coordinate well in pictures and in the reception line.

If you think this sounds too fussy for a second wedding, learn from me. I thought this was too "first wedding-ish" to do at my fourth wedding, so neither mother ever talked clothes to each other. My mother-in-law-to-be showed up in a glamorous *white* suit; my mother appeared in the *identical* suit, only in a passionate shade of fuchsia. They stood there next to each other during the ceremony, looking for all the world like twin bridesmaids. They each handled the situation with great grace, and they both looked absolutely stunning. But they would probably have rather worn different dresses. If either you or your fiancé has a stepmother, give her the courtesy of a call, too, since she'll also be in the photos. Black is not an appropriate choice for any of them, unless you are planning a "black-and-white" wedding. The mother's dresses should be a similar length and degree of formality.

If your fiancé and his best man and ushers are wearing tuxedoes, your fathers may wear tuxedoes, too, if they like. Dark dress suits are also appropriate for dads.

What Do Guests Wear?

There used to be an ironclad rule that female wedding guests *never* wore white or ivory. I like this rule because it honors the bride—guests reserve these special colors for her. Black, although elegant and polished, is not a color of celebration, so is not appropriate as wedding wear.

If a guest breaks this rule, ignore the unintentional slight.

Dress Codes

Although there are formal rules about who wears what to weddings given at certain times of day, you and your guests needn't feel bound by them. The rules are dated and getting more so by the hour. But, they are meant to help the wedding party, family, and bride be coordinated in the same degree of formality and to offer helpful guidance to guests who wish to dress respectfully. If you have any questions, ask your bridal shop associate or the guy in the tuxedo shop, if he's not 19 years old.

Bridal magazine editors and bridal salon managers agree: The bride should wear what she feels comfortable and beautiful wearing.

Theme Weddings

One of the most delightful things about second weddings is that couples have usually developed a sense of humor by this time. This sense of humor sometimes leads to a funky and often fun idea: a theme wedding. One couple who both loved music from the 1940s dressed in retro style and asked their guests to do the same. Another couple who were both especially proud of their Celtic ancestry dressed in kilts and medieval-style gowns. If a theme wedding appeals to you, be sure you include enough information in your invitation so that your guests can participate if they wish.

Daytime Wedding Attire

FORMAL	*Bride* Floor-length wedding gown, a headpiece of flowers or a hats, gloves are optional
	Bridesmaids Floor-length matching gowns with matching shoes, headpieces are optional, gloves only if the bride wears gloves
	Groom, best man, ushers Cutaway coats, striped trousers, gray waistcoats, white shirts with turndown collars, striped four-in-hand ties, gray gloves, black shoes
	Mother, mother-in-law, stepmother Dresses no longer than the bride's and hats with or without a short veil, gloves are optional
	Your children If in the wedding party, age-appropriate clothes in the same level of formality as the brides-maids' and groomsmen's; if not in the wedding party, can dress as formally as the wedding party but no less formally than the guests; dress young children nicely but comfortably (or bring a change of clothes to the reception)
	Female guests Street-length cocktail or afternoon dresses that are not black, white, or ivory; gloves and hats are optional

Daytime Wedding Attire

INFORMAL (continued)	*Male guests* Dark suits with ties
SEMIFORMAL	*Bride* Floor-length white or pastel gown, a headpiece and gloves are optional
	Bridesmaids Same as formal daytime
	Groom, best man, ushers Black coats, gray waistcoats, white pleated shirts with turn-down collars or white shirts with four-in-hand ties, gray gloves, black shoes
	Mother, mother-in-law, stepmother Dresses no longer than the bride's, hats and gloves are optional
	Your children Same as formal daytime
	Female guests Street-length cocktail or afternoon dresses that are not black, white, or ivory; hats in church are optional
	Male guests Dark suits with ties
INFORMAL	*Bride* Long dress, street-length cocktail dress, or suit

INFORMAL (*continued*)	*Bridesmaids* Follow the bride: long dresses, street-length cocktail dresses, or suits *Groom, best man, ushers* If the bride wears a long dress, tuxedoes; if the bride wears a cocktail dress or suit, dark suits in winter or light suits in summer *Mother, mother-in-law, stepmother* Street-length cocktail or afternoon dresses *Your children* Same as formal daytime *Female guests* Street-length cocktail or afternoon dresses that are not black, white, or ivory *Male guests* Dark suits with ties; in summer, light trousers with dark blazers

When pulling your gown on over your head, cover your makeup with a tissue or a towel. Better yet, step into your dress.

Outdoor Wedding Wear

Sometimes geography dictates special wedding clothes. If you are getting married on a beach, you and your wedding party are obviously going to wear casual clothes (and maybe even go barefoot!). Let your guests in on what you'll be wearing, so they can dress accordingly. If your best friend from college shows up in a Chanel suit and you're wearing a bikini top and a sarong, she'll be crabby. Plus, her heels will keep sinking into the sand.

> **HOW WE DID IT**
> I couldn't wear a headpiece; my hair is too short for that. And I hardly ever wear a dress. I live in jeans. So I chose something that was dressy and special, but still felt like "me." I found a street-length dress in a pretty, flowing fabric. I felt beautiful.
> —*Kathy, 40*

❧ Dᴏɴ'ᴛ ❧

+ Don't set up a power struggle between you and your children over clothes. Hey, at least they're willing to come to the wedding!

+ Don't fret too much about fashion rules. If you're wearing something that makes you feel beautiful, then you're doing it right.

- Don't forget to try bridal salons for dresses, even if you don't want a bridal gown; today, salons offer many choices, even nontraditional ones.

- Don't ask people what the rules are; you're inventing the rules that are right for you.

- Don't wear a blusher veil; it's a symbol of virginity, just for first-time brides.

Evening Wedding Attire	
FORMAL	*Bride* Same as formal daytime wedding, jewelry may be more "evening," if desired
	Bridesmaids Same as formal daytime
	Groom, best man, ushers Black tails and trousers, white waistcoats, shirts with wing collars, white bow ties, white gloves, black shoes
	Mother, mother-in-law, stepmother Floor-length evening gowns or dressy cocktail dresses, hats with or without veils, gloves are optional
	Your children Same as formal daytime
	Female guests Floor-length gowns or cocktail dresses, hats and gloves are optional

Evening Wedding Attire

FORMAL (continued)	**Male guests** If the women wear long dresses, tuxedoes; if the women wear short dresses, dark suits
SEMIFORMAL	**Bride** Same as semiformal daytime
	Bridesmaids Long dresses only if the bride's dress is long; same as semiformal daytime
	Groom, best man, ushers In winter, black tuxedoes; in summer, white jackets; shirts (pleated or not), black cummerbunds and bow ties, no gloves, black shoes
	Mother, mother-in-law, stepmother Same as semiformal daytime
	Your children Same as formal daytime
	Female guests Cocktail dresses, hat and gloves optional for church
	Male guests Dark suits
INFORMAL	**Bride** Street-length afternoon dress, cocktail dress, or suit

Evening Wedding Attire

INFORMAL *(continued)*	**Bridesmaids** Same style as the bride's, never longer in length than the bride's
	Groom, *best man, ushers* In winter, dark suits; in summer, dark trousers with white jackets or white trousers with navy or dark gray jackets; four-in-hand ties or other ties
	Mother, *mother-in-law, stepmother* Street-length afternoon or cocktail dresses
	Your children Same as fomal daytime
	Female guests Street-length afternoon dresses, hats and gloves optional for church
	Male guests Dark suits or light trousers and dark blazers in summer

❖ If you use a personal shopper to help you buy business clothes, call her up. Enlist her help in finding you a choice of wedding-appropriate suits, dresses, and gowns.

❖ Don't forget the internet! Key in the name of your favorite bridal or formalwear designer and search for a website. Most designers have them, and even out-of-town bridesmaids can get online with you and help choose dresses. Some choices for you and your fiancé:

❖ www.davidsbridal.com

❖ www.houseofbianchi.com

❖ www.weddingpages.com

❖ www.marisabridals.com

❖ www.watters.com

❖ www.gingiss.com

❖ www.alfredangelo.com

❖ www.dessy.com

❖ www.theknot.com/diamondbride.html

❖ www.moniquebridal.com

❖ www.emmebridal.com

❖ www.cristinaarzuaga.com

Wedding Gown and Bridesmaid Gown Worksheet

Your bridal shop	
Your sales associate	
Phone number	

BRIDESMAIDS

Name	
Size	
Pantyhose size	
Shoe size	
Glove size	
Name	
Size	
Pantyhose size	
Shoe size	
Glove size	

Wedding Gown and Bridesmaid Gown Worksheet

BRIDESMAIDS

Name	
Size	
Pantyhose size	
Shoe size	
Glove size	
Name	
Size	
Pantyhose size	
Shoe size	
Glove size	
Name	
Size	
Pantyhose size	
Shoe size	
Glove size	

CHAPTER ELEVEN

YOUR HONEYMOON
AND LIVING HAPPILY
EVER AFTER

You Did It!

You're married! Your wedding and reception were glorious and are now happy memories.

❧ TIP ❧

You now have at least one terrific shot of you and your children, all dressed up and clean. Turn it into your next holiday card, or have reprints made and send them out to each wedding guest.

Wedding Cleanup and Historic Preservation

To keep your memories preserved, assign someone to do these tasks for you after your wedding while you are away on your honeymoon:

1. Collect all your clothing, makeup, and other belongings from the bride's changing room at your ceremony site and from your reception and bring it to your home.

2. If your gown is a traditional wedding gown, bring it to a cleaner that specializes in cleaning and storing wedding gowns. Ask your bridal salon for a recommendation and for advice about how and where to store your gown.

3. If your gown is a cocktail dress or formal gown that you may wear again, bring it to cleaner immediately and return it to your closet.

4. If you'd like to preserve your wedding bouquet, your husband's boutonniere, and your children's flowers, ask your florist for advice on how best to dry your particular flowers and ask a friend to collect and treat your flowers. Later, you may display them in your home.

5. Don't accidentally donate your cake-cutting knife and server to your reception site! Ask a friend to bring them home, clean them, and return them to you.

6. Ask your maid of honor to bring your wedding certificate home with her and then return it to you when your honeymoon is over. Put it in your safety deposit box.

7. Appoint one or two people to be the "last ones out." Ask them to check the rooms at your wedding site and at your reception site, collect any articles left behind, and return them to you after your honeymoon.

Planning Your Honeymoon

Your wedding and reception plans may seem so demanding and detailed that plans for your honeymoon take a back seat. Try to find time to set aside a few hours here and there to daydream with your fiancé about your ideal honeymoon and to see if you can make your dreams a reality.

Choose a spot

Bridal magazines are filled with advertisements for popular honeymoon destinations. If you'd rather not be surrounded by 25-year-olds, choose a place that is special to you and your fiancé. If you can't afford a trip to a tropical island or an exotic resort, investigate the romantic destinations in your home state. Is there a Victorian bed-and-breakfast with a room with a double whirlpool? Is there a health and beauty spa for couples? Does the top hotel in town have a honeymoon suite? Whatever you decide, don't forget that where you are isn't as important as the fact that you're together.

> **HOW WE DID IT**
> We didn't pack our wedding-cake knife and server away. We keep it with our dishes and use them at our children's birthdays, our anniversary, special events, and any night when we serve cake or pie. The kids love it, and it gives us a very happy memory.
> —*Michelle, 37*

Don't go back to the site of your first honeymoon

One of my exes once arranged a family "honeymoon" shortly after our wedding. We traveled to a lovely north-woods condominium, which turned into the most miserable week of our lives. He was depressed, the kids were weepy, and it took three days for him to admit to me that this was where he and his first wife had often vacationed with the kids. It was also the place where she first told him she had just been diagnosed with cancer.

What was he thinking? Well, probably nothing more ominous than, "Gee, we used to have fun at this place as a family. I'll take my new family there, and we'll have fun, too."

You may think that these things, which made you happy once, will make you happy again. Instead, they may turn you into a melancholy mess. A surprising number of remarrying couples actually consider returning to a previous honeymoon spot. Don't do it! Use your imagination. Use your travel agent. Use the honeymoon section of a bride's magazine. Think of a new place!

Consider a delayed honeymoon

If out-of-town friends and family will be around for a few days after the wedding, you may want to postpone your honeymoon to allow time to visit with special people you don't often get to see. This isn't typical among young newlyweds, but older second-timers often cherish an opportunity to spend time with lifelong friends. Make sure this is a *mutual* choice of both you and your fiancé. Then make postwedding social plans for the day or two following your wedding.

Another reason for a brief delay in leaving on your honeymoon: If your children have been tense about what this new marriage means, seeing you the next morning can only reassure them. Postponing the trip for a few days may help them adjust.

Visualize together

In much the same manner that you first imagined your wedding and reception options, talk together about what style of honeymoon you would like.

- ◈ Do you want an active honeymoon, filled with sporting activities like golf and snorkeling?

- ◈ Do you want to explore a part of the country you've never seen before?

- ◈ Do you want a honeymoon filled with cultural events, like concerts and theater?

- ◈ Do you want a honeymoon of constant traveling, or do you want to go to one destination and stay there?

- ◈ Do you want to snuggle into a house or cabin and cook for yourselves, or do you want to go out to dinner every night?

Budget stretchers

- ◈ If your wedding is in the off-season for a popular vacation destination, take advantage of the low rates.

- ◈ Buy your transportation tickets early enough to take advantage of discounts.

- ◈ Check into package deals at resorts and clubs.

Sketch out a budget

Start your honeymoon budget conversation with your fiancé by filling out this form.

Honeymoon Budget Worksheet	
	ESTIMATE COSTS FOR
Transportation to and from	
Room rates	
Meals	
Liquor	
Entertainment (stage shows, snorkeling, greens fees)	
Tips	
Taxes	
Kennel for pets you leave behind	
Baby-sitter for the children	
House sitter	

Your honeymoon trousseau

The idea of accumulating a trousseau for your new life as a wife is a slightly old-fashioned one. You've probably been buying your own clothes for years! Still, getting remarried is a logical time to clean closets and put everyday systems in order. The months ahead will be busy and filled with parties, shopping, and many meetings. This can be a fun time to plan ahead, consider the clothing items you'll be needing, and shop for them in an organized way.

If you are planning a honeymoon trip with your new husband, shop ahead during the "slower" months of wedding planning for your honeymoon clothes and lingerie. If you leave this shopping until the last minute, you'll be stressed and preoccupied with relatives, parties, and wedding details.

Remember to plan or purchase a "going away" outfit for traveling from your reception to the hotel or airport.

If you are also planning a trip with your children, add the vacation clothing they need to your list. Take the kids along and make these fun outings in which you get a chance to talk together about how your lives are changing. Encourage them to ask questions and find excuses to spend "just Mom and me" time with each of them.

Pack the essentials

Your style of honeymoon will dictate your clothing choices. In addition to your daytime wardrobe, pack:

- Gorgeous lingerie

- Bubble bath

- A terrific-looking silk robe

- Matching bras and panties

- Pretty slippers (not those fluffy, scruffy ones you wear around the house)

- Makeup

- A photo ID for each of you

- Prescription medications

- Birth control

- Spare contacts and/or eyeglasses

- Health insurance card

- CDs of music to make love by

If your honeymoon destination is a foreign country, check with your travel agent for specifics. You'll probably need:

- Everything just listed

- Your passport

- Your fiancé's passport

- Traveler's checks

- Sunscreen

Should Your Children Go on Your Honeymoon?

Perhaps this is a horrid idea, but there's a kernel of wisdom in it. If your children and stepchildren-to-be are stewing about your marriage, and the first consequence of your marriage is that they all get dumped with a baby-sitter for a boring week of missing their parents and feeling left out, what have you wrought?

Certainly, you and your new husband deserve a romantic honeymoon on your own without your children along. In fact, time alone is a survival skill for stepparents. Keep scheduling it and honoring it in the coming years.

Consider planning a fun family trip or event in addition to your private honeymoon. Then you can tell the kids, "Tom and I will be taking a little trip on our own, but when we come back, we'll all be going to . . ." This family trip will make your absence a less bitter pill to swallow and will give your new blended family a fun event that celebrates your new life together.

Your Children Should Enjoy Your Honeymoon, Too

For honeymoon success, be sure to make baby-sitter plans that your children will enjoy. A week with Dad or with Grandma may be eagerly anticipated, but a week with crabby Aunt Ethel will earn you nothing but trouble (and late-night phone calls from teary kids during your romantic trysts).

Choose a baby-sitter your children like and try to get the sitter to come to your home, so your children can stay in familiar surroundings. Plan their time with a sitter with input from your children and include events they can look forward to: movies with friends, pizza night, going to the airport to meet you when you return.

If you are combining two households of children, don't try to combine them for the first time while you are away and they are with a sitter (yikes!). Instead, wait until you return and then bring the children together under one roof.

Stay in Touch While You're Gone

Plan on sending individual postcards to each child while you're away. Leave a special gift for each child wrapped and in his or her room to discover after your departure. Write notes for each day that you're gone. Call home often. If your children are young, make a calendar for them to count off the days until you return. Plan a kid-focused day and night when you return. Once you're at home, consider your romantic honeymoon temporarily suspended while you both work to lay a strong foundation for a happy blended family.

After the Honeymoon

Change your name

If you or you and your fiancé are changing your name or names, include these documents, agencies, and organizations on your list of places to notify and papers to change:

- Passports
- Wills

- Voter registration

- Social security

- Stock certificates

- Your lawyer's office

- Work records

- Life insurance beneficiaries

- Car insurance provider

- Banks

- Driver's license

- Internal Revenue Service

- Post office

- School records

- Alumni listings

- Utilities

- Credit cards

- Car registration

❖ DON'T ❖

Don't forget to write a sincere thank-you note to whomever baby-sat your children while you were away on your honeymoon. Include a gift—perhaps mutual baby-sitting while *they* get away from *their* kids?

Finish your thank-you notes

Once you've returned from your honeymoon (from both of them, if you also took a trip with the kids), sit down and finish up your thank-you notes. Your new husband may certainly help you. Made sure each guest who brought you a gift receives a hand-written note from one of you.

If your parents and your in-laws helped out in any way, send them notes, too.

❧ ETIQUETTE NOTES ❧

In a thank-you note for cash, do not mention the exact amount of the check or gift. Simply say something along the lines of "Tim and I thank you for your generous gift."

Write thank-you notes to your children, too

Your children and your new stepchildren must have done *something* helpful during the weeks and months of planning your wedding. What can you thank them for? Helping you pick the tablecloth colors? Stuffing envelopes? Playing nicely with the other children at your reception? Think of something, even if you have to stretch the truth, and write loving notes to your children and stepchildren.

Starting Your New Stepfamily Life Together

Every newlywed couple has adjustments to make as they work through the first few months (and years!) of married life. The difference with a stepfamily is that:

- You're making these awkward adjustments right in front of your children.

- You're also making awkward adjustments to your stepchildren.

- Your children are making awkward adjustments to their stepsiblings and stepfather.

- Your stepchildren are making awkward adjustments to your children and to you.

Good intentions count for a lot, but sailing into this stepfamily business without adequate preparation can make for choppy seas.

Helping children adjust to postwedding life

Shirley Glass, Ph.D., a Baltimore psychologist and a relationship columnist for America Online's magazine *Oxygen*, raises a red flag on a common stepfamily danger.

"A lot of second marriages end because of the parenting of stepchildren," she says. "What often happens is this: The biological parent may be overindulging the child because of the loss of the intact family. The new person coming into the family system sees a need to create more limit setting, to focus on building character, and comes in with a missionary zeal to be the answer to everyone's prayers—except no one was praying!"

Instead of bonding with the stepchildren and creating an air of acceptance, Glass says, the stepparent often comes in and tries to make rules. And instead of the spouse joining in with the stepparent to help make new rules, the biological parent tries to compensate for the stepparent's harshness and protect the child.

The couple doesn't make it. What needs to happen, says Glass, is that the biological parent should take a slightly harder stand about behavior and discipline, and the stepparent should relax, play with the kids, and have fun. It takes four to five years to integrate a new parent into a family. "The stepparent needs to come in very gently, and really give the kids a lot of time," she says.

Here's a stepparent fairy tale that's famous in our family. The day before I was to marry my husband, Bill, I had to go to work. I was working for a national publisher then, and we were about to launch a new magazine.

Bill stepped in to handle home preparations. With me off at work, he had decided to organize wedding clothes for the children. I had already taken the kids shopping, and they had each picked out what they wanted to wear. Ian, then 9 years old, had chosen a navy blue blazer and khaki pants. Bill was excavating his way through Ian's closet, trying to find a belt and tie.

Somewhere along the way, there was an incident. Probably something like Bill saying, "You know, if you cleaned out this closet once in a while . . ." And something like Ian thinking, "Who is this guy, anyway?"

I got a phone call at the office. At first, I couldn't even hear the voice on the other end. Then, I realized it was Ian, furtively whispering into the telephone.

"Mom! Mom!" he hissed. "I have something important to tell you."

I was standing in the middle of a packed, semichaotic office, and I struggled to hear.

"Mom! You never really asked my opinion about Bill. You're getting married, and I have nothing to say about it. Well, my advice is: 'Dump him!' "

What did I do when Ian called? I moved to a quieter spot. I told Ian to go to a phone in the house where he didn't have to whisper. I told him whatever he told me, I would keep in the strictest confidence and never tell Bill. And then, I listened while he poured out his heart. I told him I understood that today felt pretty scary. I asked Ian to keep trying to tell Bill how he felt until I could get home. I told Ian to think of Bill today as a baby-sitter and to mind Bill until I could be there. And then I left the office early and went home. First things first.

By the time I got there, everything was fine. I did not make my appearance seem like I had dashed home in a panic because Ian blew the whistle. When I had a chance, I took Bill aside and reminded him that we might expect the kids to act out their anxiety about the wedding in a variety of ways over the next few days. Bill, who has no children of his own, learned quickly. He cleared the air with Ian in a little heart-to-heart talk in front of a video game. And now, five years (and several more little scenes like this) later, Ian and Bill are close and affectionate.

Will I ever get time alone with Mom again?

Your children may accept your new marriage more gracefully if it doesn't bring their own relationship with you to a screeching halt. If you and your son always spent Sunday afternoons at the zoo, keep heading for the lion cages, just the two of you. If you and your daughter made the last half hour before bedtime your private cuddle-and-talk time, then stick with it and don't invite your husband—for a while, at least.

Maintaining the closeness you have with your children, while adding your husband as an extra plus, can sidestep friction and resentment later on.

❧ KIDS TALK ❧

There should always be a little mother-daughter time. I don't always want my stepfather around, even though I love him.
—*Hannah, 9*

I like my stepdad

"I've seen some beautiful stepparent relationships," says Cecelia Soares, a marriage and family therapist and seminar speaker. "That's a real tribute to the maturity of the stepparent. The child is testing you: 'Are you a grown-up? Can you handle this? Can I trust you to know what to do?' If you can react with maturity, you pass the test."

Soares urges stepparents to set limits firmly, but fairly. "You're a kind of parent, but not a parent, so you can't really lay down the law," she says. "You're a person, though, so you can ask for the kind of behavior around you that you can tolerate."

Rather than "In this house, we keep our rooms clean, young man!" try "I'd like to chat, but I can't concentrate in a messy room. You straighten this up, I'll go downstairs and make root beer floats, and let's meet on the porch."

Says Soares, "You can't shoehorn a new person into a family by force. You have to give the new person and the children lots of time and let it happen gently. You really need to be the best you can be in terms of being an adult. You can't come home and kick off your shoes and react however you want to—you're modeling adult reactions for children."

Rough times

The first weeks and months of your marriage may be a honeymoon with your new stepchildren, or they may be rough going, indeed. Try to find creative ways to diffuse the strong emotions swirling around your house. You may be surprised to realize that you don't always need to provide answers as much as you need to provide a sympathetic ear and understanding.

Power to the children

Children may also try to establish ground rules with you. Acknowledge what they are trying to say, and if you can, agree with them. You're the adult. That means you're the one who

Ways to Respond to a Cranky Stepchild

CHILD SAYS	YOU SAY
"I don't want you here. I miss my mom."	"You really miss your mom. When I'm here, it feels worse."
"I wish you'd just leave."	"You like it better when it's just you and Dad alone here."
"You're not any fun."	"We're not doing anything fun yet. What could we do now that would be fun?"

is supposed to understand, give, yield, and extend yourself. No kidding.

A secret that an experienced stepmother told me long ago has guided me through the years (and through several adolescents!): "Whenever you can, let your child have control of something."

Green-eyed monsters

Imagine how upsetting it is to your stepchild to realize that suddenly, Dad is no longer *her* champion, but *your* champion. This is prime ground for jealousy, and few children can escape feeling it. Dad can help by maintaining special, private time with his children, by lovingly supporting you in front of all your children, and by not mocking or embarrassing your children.

At first, I thought my stepfather was really cool. Then, he started getting bossy, and I didn't like him so much. I hate it when he talks about my father, even if he says nice things. Now, I guess he's OK.

—*Andrew, 11*

Tantrum treatments

Crying, yelling, and throwing tantrums are behaviors that embarrass most people who try them, once they recover and remember how foolish they were. Children often feel this way, too. It's one thing to act out in front of your family; it's another to act out in front of kids you don't know well (your new stepsiblings) and in front of a perfect stranger (you or your husband). So when things get emotional, try to extend respect to your child:

- Don't laugh.

- Don't say anything insulting, mocking, or degrading.

- Establish eye contact and wear a serious, concerned expression.

- Offer to take matters behind closed doors, away from the siblings.

- Listen to the ranting until you understand the basic issue. Then say something respectful, like "Boy, I sure hear that you are really, really upset. I'd like to listen to everything that is upsetting you until you feel like I've really heard you. Do you want a little more time to calm down, first, or would you like to start talking together now?"

But I want them to love me

You want to be a perfect stepmother and have perfect stepchildren who adore you instantly. Well, we all do. But you can't force his children to love you, and your husband can't force your children to love him. If you are both reliable, sincere, and patient, you may be surprised. Someday, that snotty little stepkid will fall down, scrape a knee, and run to you for a hug and a Band-Aid.

How to Help a Child Feel in Control

CHILD SAYS	YOU SAY
"You're not the boss of me."	"You're right. I am not the boss of you. You have to mind Dad, not me."
"You're not my father."	"You're right. You already have a father, and a good one. I'm sort of extra."
"This is my house; it isn't your house."	"This is your house, and you don't like sharing it. I don't blame you. That's a hard thing to do."
"You can't come in my room."	"You like your room to be your own private space. OK. I'll knock, and I won't come in unless you invite me."

After three dreadful months of trying to adjust calmly to my stepson, Seth, and get him to like me, I finally snapped one day and yelled, "You're right! I'm not your mother! I can't boss you around and I can't tell you what to do! But I can drive you to soccer, and I can take you out for a hamburger, and I can tell you how to talk to that girl in English class, so how about it?" Seth gave me a startled look, and then said, "Well, OK." That moment didn't fix everything, but I really think it helped.

—*Jane, 36*

In the meantime, try to ignore the bratty behavior and implement some behaviors of your own that kids tend to like.

Make friends with your stepchildren

- Ask about their interests and really listen.

- Ask them to teach you how to play a video game.

- Invite them to do something together ("let's play chess," "let's go shopping").

- Stand up for them ("Wait a minute—Joshua said he doesn't want Chinese tonight. Let's think of another restaurant.").

- Spend time with them without showing signs of impatience or boredom.

- Let them make a grown-up decision ("Heather, you decide which way we drive home tonight," "Adam, should we go to the hardware store or the garden store first?").

- Honor their requests. If little Johnny has asked three times to be taken to the new movie about space aliens, and his exhausted father has overlooked his request, you be the hero. Make a date with Johnny. Maybe invite Dad, maybe not.

Gross! They're kissing!

Two newlyweds with stars in their eyes are one thing. But when they're both 42 and sitting at the kitchen table mooning at each other right in front of their teenage son, it's gross.

You'll be hugging, kissing, giggling, and holding hands—at least, if you're doing it right, you will be. Be aware that this behavior can upset young children, who may view it as you being disloyal to their dad or as their dad being disloyal to their mom. Teenagers, who are busy trying to figure out their own sexuality, may be embarrassed by grownups expressing physical affection.

> **HOW WE DID IT**
> I always thought her son hated me until one day he invited me to come to his school program and introduced me as his friend.
> —*Sam, 44*

If you get some strong reactions, stay affectionate toward each other, but tone down the heavier stuff until you're behind closed doors—for a while. As your new relationships with his children, and his with yours, grow and develop, the children may begin to enjoy seeing you two relating so sweetly to each other.

Helping Grown Children
Adjust to Postwedding Life

Remember when your children left home and you needed to renegotiate your relationship with them in an adult-to-adult way? Now, there is another renegotiation at work. You've added a new person to the family, and your grown children must negotiate a new relationship with you (because you don't live alone anymore) and a new relationship with your spouse.

Chances are, your grown children are delighted that you've found happiness again and wish you the best. But when you sense uneasiness in them or friction between them and your husband, there are things you can do to relieve the tension. And, if there is friction between you and your grown stepchildren, both you and your husband can address it.

Plain talk about money

Your children and stepchildren may be wondering how your new marriage will affect family property, their inheritance, and their children's inheritance. They are almost surely wondering if your new husband will get all Dad's insurance money, if his name is now on the deed to the family homestead, and if you've changed your will to include him and cut them out. They may feel these thoughts are too mercenary to voice, but they are probably having them just the same.

Before you blame them for being selfish, remember that money matters are seldom actually about money. What your children are really wondering is: "Has this guy just cut us out of our own family? Does Mom love him more than us? Was our family, as we knew it, just destroyed? And is Mom happy about it?" They don't want your money as much as they want reassurance that you love them and that they are still central in your life.

One of the best steps you can take is to sit down with your children (without your husband) and review family finances. If their father died, go over where his money is now and how much of it will go to them when you die. Show them your plans for the future. Explain your life insurance beneficiary arrangements, the terms of your will, and your intentions for the outcome of your property.

Simply learning what you have planned and how you have safeguarded at least some family property and inheritance for them and their children may significantly ease stepfamily tension.

Are you going to change things?

Your grown stepchildren may have spent their entire childhood in the home you've now moved into with your new husband. They may feel it's more theirs than yours. They may resent any change you suggest, from covering up old wallpaper ("My mother hung that herself!") to using an old bedroom as an office ("This has always been a guest room!").

Try to find ways to tell them that you appreciate what's hard about this change and initiate conversations. "Tom, I was thinking about making a change to the house, but I don't want to offend you or your sister. What would you think if . . ." Confess to them that it's difficult for you to try to inhabit space that is so meaningful to all of them. They're grown-ups—they should have to understand your point of view, too.

I don't even know what bugs me about my mother's new husband. My wife keeps asking me, "What's wrong with him?" He seems to be a nice guy, and I can see that he loves my mother. But since their wedding, I don't even want to go visit Mom anymore. I'd rather she just come over here and see her grandchildren at our house.

—*Scott, 31*

Where's Dad's fishing rod?

Help both your grown children and your new husband by doing a little "estate planning." Ask your children which possessions and objects in your home have great sentimental value to them. There may be some—a desk from a childhood bedroom, a favorite piece of china—that you could part with now and give to them as gifts. For other items, make a list and let your children know that you will be specifying these arrangements in your will.

If your children know that Dad's collection of trout lures will not be going to your new husband, but to your son, tensions may ease and potential irritations may smooth away.

Childish feelings in grown-ups

Yes, your children are adults. But they are still your children, and when it comes to you, they may still have some pretty childlike feelings. They may even surprise themselves with how possessive and jealous they can get. If you can act understanding, instead of reacting in negative ways, they may outgrow this stuff—by the time they're 50 or so.

Mom, where do I fit?

Your adult children are jockeying for position, trying to figure out where they fit in your new family structure. Let them know that they *do* fit and that their reactions matter to you. Demonstrate that you are willing to help them make a space in your family unit. Ask them to help make a space for your new husband.

Your grown children deserve clear messages

All these adjustments will be easier if you are straight with your children. Tell them directly just where they stand. Outline how your new marriage affects them materially and financially and support them emotionally.

Avoid offending your adult stepchildren

If you can head off at the pass these kinds of problems with your stepchildren, do it! Ask your husband to review financial matters with his children. Ask him for clear instructions about the disposition of property and money in the event of his death. Help him sort out family heirlooms and suggest that he give each child at least one significant piece as a kind of "wedding present."

Pretty soon, those grown kids will stop calling you "that woman."

Being Married to a Man
with a Past

Getting married when you two aren't teenagers any more means that your marriage cannot escape having elements of your past relationships mixed into it. This can be an enriching experience, but it can also feel unsettling. It may sometimes feel as if you are being unfaithful to your earlier love and family. And it may sometimes feel as if you are being unfaithful to your current love and family.

In your new relationship, it's not possible for the two of you to have the sort of clean, fresh start that dewy-eyed kids just out of school have. If you and your previous spouse were married at a young age, you probably built a life together from scratch, sharing pivotal life experiences like buying your first house and having your first child.

You and your new husband will never have these experiences. When you each tell stories of starting out in life, you'll be telling stories that involve an ex. When you recall the births of your children, you'll be recalling tender moments with another spouse. You won't have years of shared history.

Embrace your separate histories

If you decide to embrace your separate histories, you'll have an easier time than if you decide to fight them. The fact that he was married before he met you really isn't a sign of infidelity. If you decide to react with jealous behavior, you've just created one of the major relationship issues you two will have to conquer. You can't blame your new love for what happened in his life before he met you—just like he can't blame you for the marriage you had before you knew he was on the planet.

You can let the past drive you crazy, or you can find a way to live with it. Consider *not* creating this an issue at all.

Don't blame each other for the past

Here's a true story:

Burt was Ramona's first husband. But Burt was married before, to Sylvia, and they had a son. Naturally, Burt and Sylvia had to talk and occasionally see each other over matters that involved 8-year-old Matt. Ramona chose to fly into jealous rages and throw temper tantrums each time she answered the telephone and heard Sylvia's voice. She blamed Burt for the time he spent with Matt, as though Burt were being unfaithful with another woman. Burt felt trapped. He loved Ramona dearly, but had no intention of abandoning his son to make Ramona feel more secure. When Ramona became pregnant, she was delighted, and told her friends, "Now Burt and I will have our own family, and he won't have to keep visiting his old one." Ramona is making herself miserable, she's probably on her way to her first divorce, and she may be having a baby for all the wrong reasons. Burt isn't being unfaithful to Ramona when he spends time with his son; he's being a good father and deserves admiration and support for that role.

Here's another way to deal with previous spouses:

Frequently, my husband, Bill, has to answer the door and find one of my ex-husbands standing there. Although these aren't guys I want to live with now, I'm glad to see them, because it means they are still involved in their children's lives—and children need the love of their fathers. Bill has never thrown a fit over the occasional presence of an ex in our lives and has always reacted to their presence with grace. He knows that the ex is here for paternal reasons, not romantic ones. And he realizes that his stepchildren need to see him being polite to their fathers. That's why our complicated blended family works.

Create your new future together

Though you may not have a shared history, you and your new husband will have the new experiences of blending your histories and creating a new life for yourselves. And you can share a respect for each other's histories. After all, his previous life experiences have made him the man you love today!

Have a wonderful, loving life together! Congratulations!

❧ RESOURCES ❧

The Stepfamily Association of America
215 Centennial Mall South, Suite 212
Lincoln, NE 68508
(800) 735-0329
(402) 477-STEP

National Council on Family Relations
3989 Central Avenue NE, Suite 550
Minneapolis, MN 55421
(612) 781-9331

CHAPTER TWELVE

YOUR PLANNING CALENDAR

For Your Wedding, Reception, and Honeymoon

Second weddings are rarely planned as far in advance as are first weddings. However, if you can give yourselves several months, you may feel more relaxed and find that you actually enjoy the planning and arranging. More important, you'll have more time to prepare your children and your future stepchildren.

This checklist is organized in order of the tasks you'll need to do first. Since florists, photographers, churches and temples, and musicians are often booked months in advance, this wedding checklist begins six to twelve months before your wedding. If you don't have that much time, you can still start at the beginning and work your way through the list.

All these points are covered in more detail in specific, earlier chapters.

Carry this book in your briefcase or purse. Over the next

months, you'll be trying to plan a wedding in the moments between business meetings, transporting children to and from school events, and living your already busy life. If you keep this book with you, you can use a ten-minute wait at your daughter's soccer game to phone your florist or to schedule a dress fitting.

One year to six months before your wedding

____ 1. Before you do anything else, discuss your engagement with your children and your fiancé's children.

____ 2. Once your children know and have had a chance to air their grievances and delight at the prospect, *then* announce your engagement to the rest of your family and friends.

____ 3. Start weighing your options and talking together about where you're all going to live (that's probably your children's first question, anyway).

____ 4. Discuss general wedding day options with your fiancé. Fill out the **Wedding Day Options Worksheet in Chapter Four.** Once you settle on a way that you both want your wedding to *feel* as an event, your decisions about food, flowers, dress, and decoration will all follow.

____ 5. If you wish to hire a wedding planner or event coordinator to do some or all of your wedding and reception planning, interview and hire one now.

____ 6. Set the date and hour of the wedding.

____ 7. Book your site for the wedding ceremony and the rehearsal (if you're having one). Use the **Wedding Site and Celebrant Interview Worksheet in Chapter Six.**

_____ 8. Book your celebrant. Most celebrants want to meet with you and your fiancé before the ceremony to discuss wedding details and perhaps even your relationship and preparedness for marriage. Set the meeting date now, as well. Use the **Wedding Site and Celebrant Interview Worksheet** in Chapter Six.

_____ 9. Book your reception site. Use the **Reception Site Worksheet** in Chapter Eight.

_____ 10. If either your wedding or reception site needs special parking arrangements for your guests (such as valets, reserved spots, or a police officer), make those arrangements now.

_____ 11. Book your photographer/videographer. Don't delay! Good photographers can be booked a year in advance. Use the **Photographer/Videographer Interview Worksheet** in Chapter Seven.

_____ 12. If your reception will be catered, interview and book a caterer now. Use the **Caterer Interview Worksheet** in Chapter Eight.

_____ 13. Choose a florist and reserve your date. Use the **Florist Interview Worksheet** in Chapter Seven.

_____ 14. Arrange for music before, during, and after the ceremony. Use the **Your Music Choices Worksheet** in Chapter Seven.

_____ 15. Arrange for reception music. Use the **Musician Interview Worksheet** in Chapter Seven.

_____ 16. As you're booking, if you run into snags, go back to your **Wedding Day Options Worksheet** in Chapter Four. Could you be flexible about any of your choices?

_____ 17. Discuss with your children and/or his children how each would like to be involved in your wedding.

_____ 18. *After* you've planned special roles for your children and his children, *then* select the other members of the wedding party. (If you ask your lifelong best friend to be maid of honor before you talk with your daughter and discover this is her heart's desire, you've got a sticky problem.)

_____ 19. If your parents or his parents have expressed an interest in helping with the wedding and reception plans, discuss their expectations. If his mother or yours is counting on as much involvement in the guest list and caterering arrangements as in the first wedding, it's better to learn that up front before you get too far along in your planning.

_____ 20. Many remarrying couples finance their own wedding, but your parents or his may wish to contribute. If they've offered, settle on a specific way they may help: picking up the liquor tab, donating the cake, hosting the rehearsal dinner, and so forth.

_____ 21. Work with your caterer on menus. Include choices appropriate for vegetarian/vegan guests and for your children.

_____ 22. Ask your caterer when a final count of the number of guests is needed and note that day on your calendar to remind you.

_____ 23. If you wish to let your parents and your fiancé's parents invite guests, ask them how many invitations they'll need.

_____ 24. Start drawing up your guest list.

_____ 25. Start a beauty regimen (and nutritious eating with lots of water, while you're at it) to look and feel your best during this demanding time. Keep a regular skin-care program, including facials. Start using teeth-whitening toothpaste and/or ask your dentist for a whitening program. Sleep, sleep, sleep!

____ 26. If your ceremony and/or reception is to be held in your home or garden, walk through it now and make a list of all the repairs, painting, planting, cleaning, and other work to be done. Make a fun family project out of some of this work by making a chart on the refrigerator that measures your progress toward "our wedding." (Just don't create grudges by turning the children into wedding slaves. Keep it fun. If your stepdaughter-to-be hates painting, ask her to help choose colors with you, instead.)

____ 27. Talk to your children about how to make the reception fun for them.

____ 28. Arrange transportation to get:
____You and your children to the wedding
____Your fiancé and his children to the wedding
____Members of the wedding party to the wedding
____Parents and grandparents to the wedding
____You, your fiancé, and all children from the wedding to the reception
____Members of the wedding party from the wedding to the reception
____Parents and grandparents from the wedding to the reception
____Hint: Even the most recalcitrant stepchild may perk up at the prospect of a limousine ride! Ask the limousine service to stock the car with juice, water, and soft drinks to keep the children hydrated and happy throughout the day.

____ 29. Begin visiting bakeries to choose the flavor and style of your wedding cake.

_____ 30. Get ready to go dress shopping: buy a strapless bustier, decent panties, and shoes at a height you like for trying on dresses. Once you've chosen your gown, you can buy real lingerie and shoes that match.

_____ 31. Shop for your dress and veil or hat.

_____ 32. Shop for your shoes and accessories.

_____ 33. Start breaking in your shoes.

_____ 34. Shop for your children's clothes. It's best to talk about the kind of clothes and get a general agreement from the children ahead of time, but don't buy anything until shortly before the ceremony, or you may find that your children have just outgrown their new designer outfit.

_____ 35. Purchase or arrange to rent your groom's tuxedo or suit.

_____ 36. Decide on clothes for the wedding party. If you wish to have bridesmaids in similar dresses, choose them immediately after you've chosen your own dress, to allow time for ordering and fittings. Notify the bridesmaids of where to go to be fitted and how to order their dresses. If you have a small wedding party choosing dress clothes off the rack, arrange for them to shop together and allow enough time for special orders, if necessary. If the best man and ushers are to wear tuxedoes, your fiancé should inform them of where to go to be measured and to order. Each member of the wedding party pays for his or her own clothes. Discussing a price range ahead of time is thoughtful.

_____ 37. If your bridesmaids are to wear matching shoes, order them at once and have them dyed in the same dye lot.

____ 38. Go ahead, be a perfectionist—buy the same shade of pantyhose for each bridesmaid. You'd be surprised how odd different-colored legs can look in wedding pictures! While you're at it, buy lipsticks and nail polish in matching colors.

____ 39. Let your mother and the groom's mother know what you, your children, and the wedding party have chosen to wear, so they can choose their dresses accordingly. Your mother chooses her dress first and then lets the groom's mother know.

____ 40. Stock up on thank-you notes and use them for people who help you run errands and handle details, as well as for those who give you shower and early wedding gifts. If you use monogrammed personal stationery, use your current monogram until your wedding. For thank-you notes sent after your wedding, it's appropriate to use the monogram or name you'll assume after you're married.

____ 41. Consider sending out a preinvitation notification of your wedding date. This notification isn't traditional, but busy people sometimes need advance notice to make room on their calendars. You may phone family members and special guests to ask them to hold the date or dash off a quick, informal note.

____ 42. Choose your rings.

____ 43. Register for gifts.

____ 44. Finalize your guest list.

____ 45. Choose and order your wedding invitations.

____ 46. Discuss your honeymoon options. Consider taking two trips: one with your new husband and one with your children, celebrating your new family.

____ 47. Check with the wedding party to be sure they have ordered their dresses and tuxedoes.

_____ 48. Plan your honeymoon trousseau. Schedule time to shop for your going-away outfit (if other than your wedding gown) and honeymoon wardrobe. If you're taking a family trip, include time to shop for the children.

_____ 49. Send invitations four to eight weeks before your wedding.

_____ 50. Make appointments for the children to get caught up on dentists' and doctors' appointments before the wedding. This may help offset an emergency or health problem while you are on your honeymoon.

_____ 51. Schedule your own physical, teeth cleaning, and dental checkup about four to six weeks before your wedding. If your state requires a blood test before marriage, tell the receptionist when you schedule your doctor's visit. Be sure to schedule your blood test to occur during the period required by your state (if it's too far ahead of your wedding, you may have to repeat it).

_____ 52. Schedule haircut appointments for the children now to get the day and time most convenient for you just before the wedding.

_____ 53. Schedule a spa day, if your budget allows, for you to get a good massage, pedicure, and manicure a few days before the wedding.

_____ 54. Schedule a hair appointment for yourself for the day before or day of the wedding.

_____ 55. Decide if you want guests to toss rice, birdseed, flower petals, or paper flower petals when you leave your reception. Order ribbon-tied bags now and ask someone (a young cousin, one of your children, a friend's child) to pass them out to guests on your wedding day.

____ 56. When the invitations arrive, address them. Plan on enough time to do this task. Hand addressing outer and inner envelopes can be time consuming.

____ 57. If you wish to have a wedding program, write the text and have it printed or produce it on a laser printer.

____ 58. Look at your business calendar for the weeks before your wedding. Cancel or move any business appointments that you can. Lighten your workload for the month before your wedding and consider taking vacation time. If you need to, inform business associates or your employer of the time you'll be taking off.

Three to five months before your wedding

____ 1. Start planning what your ceremony will be like. What readings do you want? What music? Are there special ethnic or religious touches you want to add?

____ 2. Draw sketches of your wedding site arrangements. Where do you want flowers, candles, ribbons? Where will your families sit? Where will your wedding party assemble and enter? What will their formation be at the altar? Where will your celebrant stand? How will you exit? If your receiving line is to be at the church or temple, where will you stand?

____ 3. Sketch out your reception site arrangements. Allow for a cake table, guest tables, food tables, gift tables, a guest book signing table, a punch table, a bar, and guest chairs and tables. Discuss where to place flowers brought from the wedding.

___ 4. Decide on decorations for the guest tables at the reception site and enlist help in preparing them.

___ 5. Decide if you want to have a gift table. If so, arrange for someone to unwrap the gifts, display them, and keep a clear record of who gave what.

___ 6. Finalize your reception menu with the caterer. Meet with your caterer to discuss all the reception details that matter to you and to clarify which ones the caterer will be responsible for supervising. Use the **Reception Site Worksheet in Chapter Eight.**

___ 7. If your reception site has a special-event coordinator, meet with that person to discuss all the details you've planned for the reception. Use the **Reception Site Worksheet in Chapter Eight.**

___ 8. Finalize your cake choice. If possible, bring a photo of your cake style to your caterer and florist so that flowers for the cake table can be arranged. Use the **Wedding Cake Worksheet in Chapter Eight.**

___ 9. Finalize your honeymoon plans. Make transportation and hotel reservations.

___ 10. Do you have adequate honeymoon luggage? And if you have planned a family trip with the children, do you have enough luggage for the whole crew?

___ 11. Have the name discussion. Are you taking his name? Adding it on with a hyphen? If you decide to make any kind of name change, notify your insurance companies, accountant, lawyer, bank, credit card companies, and anyone else. Schedule time to have your driver's license changed soon after the wedding.

___ 12. If you're having a wedding rehearsal, plan the rehearsal dinner. If your in-laws are hosting the dinner, coordinate guest lists and seating arrangements with them. If you need to arrange for a baby-sitter for your children, reserve one now.

___ 13. If you are going to send announcements after the wedding (they only go to people you didn't invite but who need to know), order them now.

___ 14. Ask a friend or family member to oversee the guest book at your reception. This person may need to carry the book and pen to the reception and set it up on a desk or stand. Or, you may leave these items with your caterer or reception staff after you decide where the book will be placed and ask your friend or relative to stand by the book and invite guests to sign. It's a good idea to provide two pens.

___ 15. Meet with the contact person at your ceremony site to double check the dates and times of your rehearsal and your ceremony. Some ceremony sites have two or three ceremonies occurring in the same space on the same day. Ask if there is a ceremony just ahead of or behind you that may affect the timing of your flower delivery, reception line, or photographs. Share your plan of how you want the site decorated and how you want your wedding party to enter and exit.

___ 16. As shower and wedding gifts arrive, record them in your notebook or on your file cards and send thank you notes.

___ 17. If your ceremony and/or reception is to be at home, schedule a cleaning person for before and after the ceremony (or press family members and friends into service). Also arrange with a service or friends for lawn mowing, garden maintenance, and last minute bathroom touch-up cleaning.

Four to eight weeks before the wedding

_____ 1. Mail your wedding invitations all on the same day (otherwise some guests who haven't received theirs yet will think they aren't invited). Schedule the mailing so invitations arrive four to eight weeks before your wedding.

_____ 2. As shower and wedding gifts arrive, record them in your notebook or on your file cards, and send thank you notes on the spot. As crazy as life seems now, it will only get crazier *after* the wedding!

_____ 3. Check on your gown. Has it arrived? Schedule fittings.

_____ 4. Have your physical, blood test, and dental checkups. If a blood test is required in your state, your fiancé should get one now, too.

_____ 5. Take your children to the doctor and dentist, as you previously scheduled.

_____ 6. Finalize your children's wedding clothes (they shouldn't grow *too* much in a month).

_____ 7. Check children's shoes: Right size? Dressy enough? Polished? Buy extra laces.

_____ 8. Choose a wedding gift for your fiancé. A watch, cuff links, or engraved piece of jewelry are good choices.

_____ 9. Some blended families mark the wedding with a special gift to each child. Choose these gifts and have them engraved or wrapped. You could choose a gift of particular interest to each child right now, like a computer game, toy, or book, but it's a nice idea to mark this event with something the child can keep and use for years: engraved jewelry, a special watch, a beautiful reference book, a picture frame. Add a handwritten note.

____ 10. Choose gifts for your bridesmaids (earrings, a necklace, a compact) and groomsmen (cuff links, key chain, tie clip).

____ 11. If you're interested in having your wedding announcement appear in a newspaper, contact it, find out its policy, and send the appropriate information.

____ 12. If any members of your wedding party are coming in from out of town, arrange accommodations for them, if necessary.

____ 13. For the day after your wedding, your parents may wish to entertain guests who have come from out of town in a day-after brunch, luncheon, or dinner. Coordinate guest lists with them. If you and your fiancé delay leaving for your honeymoon, attend day-after events yourself.

____ 14. If your wedding is to be at home, make any special parking arrangements (valets, attendants, special permits).

____ 15. If you receive gifts from your fiancé's family members, it's nice to let his parents know who's given what, so they may mention it at the wedding.

____ 16. Check on your gown. Have final fittings.

____ 17. Buy reception dancing shoes, an evening bag, and accessories.

____ 18. Ask a friend or family member to help you dress on your wedding day. Do you need a button hook? Ask another to help your children get ready.

____ 19. Call your county to learn the local requirements for obtaining a marriage license. Schedule a time and date with your fiancé to go to the courthouse and get the license. Splurge and make reservations at your favorite restaurant for a romantic lunch afterward.

____ 20. Have a "just us" event with your children and encourage your fiancé to have one with his. A movie, a pizza, a long heart-to-heart talk that includes reassurance that "we'll still have time for 'just us.' " Then, trade kids and spend an evening getting to know your stepchildren-to-be even better.

____ 21. Throw a luncheon for you and your bridesmaids. Give them their gifts from you and a peek at your dress.

____ 22. If you are sending wedding announcements, address them now and give them to a friend to mail after your wedding.

____ 23. Call your bridal salon. Will your dress arrive on time? Schedule any fittings that may be necessary.

____ 24. Arrange for who will pick up your wedding gown and where it will be stored until the ceremony.

____ 25. Double check with the caterer—any problems?

____ 26. Double check with the florist on delivery places and times for the ceremony flowers and the reception flowers. Wedding bouquets and boutonnieres should be delivered to the site where you are dressing (this may mean two different sites: one for the bride and one for the groom). Flower decorations for the wedding ceremony must go to the ceremony site and be delivered in time to be placed correctly. Flowers for the reception should be delivered to your reception site in time to be placed correctly.

____ 27. Ask a friend or relative to collect and store your flowers after your reception. If you want your bouquet preserved, ask your florist for advice on how to do so and arrange for it to happen. If the florist needs to pick up containers and rental pieces after the wedding, designate a friend to handle this arrangement for you while you are on your honeymoon.

_____ 28. Plan how to pack and move gifts from the reception to your home. If you will be out of town, it may be best to leave the gifts at your parents' home or at another secure site. Moving the gifts may take some coordination and several cars, so plan ahead and designate friends and family members to do this chore for you.

_____ 29. Double check on the limo service and drivers you've reserved to get you and your wedding party to and from the ceremony and reception. Make sure they understand the importance of getting from the wedding to the reception promptly so the receiving line can begin.

_____ 30. Call the bakery and double check arrangements for the cake. The bakery will usually assemble the cake on the cake table at your reception, but may leave the floral decorations for the florist to arrange. Pin down who does what and make sure they know your expectations.

_____ 31. Check with your photographer/videographer. Give them a final list of the agenda of your wedding and reception and of the photos/videos you want taken.

_____ 32. Make honeymoon arrangements for your children. Include treats and fun events, like rented movies and pizza parties.

_____ 33. If you'll be away on a honeymoon, arrange for someone to mow the lawn, collect the mail, turn lights off and on, and house sit in your absence. Arrange to board any pets for both your wedding day and your honeymoon.

Two to three weeks before your wedding

____ 1. Call the hotel where you'll be spending your wedding night and order champagne and snacks (or some other romantic surprise) for your room.

____ 2. If your children will have their own room for the night, stock it with snacks and drinks.

____ 3. Open a joint bank account if you're going to have one.

____ 4. Pick up your wedding gown.

____ 5. Check with your bridesmaids. Have they picked up their dresses and shoes?

____ 6. Write out the checks for the celebrant, musicians, caterer, florist, and others ahead of time. Put them in labeled envelopes and ask the best man to deliver them before or after the ceremony and reception.

____ 7. Plan where you, your fiancé, your children, and your wedding party will dress for the ceremony.

____ 8. Review special seating arrangements in reserved pews with your guests and your ushers. Arrange with your florist to "rope off" those seats with flowers or ribbon.

____ 9. As shower and wedding gifts arrive, record them in your notebook or on your file cards and send thank you notes.

____ 10. Call your caterer with the final guest count.

____ 11. Double check with the baby-sitter and/or entertainers who will be with your children during the wedding and reception. Be sure they understand that if they cancel, they've ruined your wedding. You may even schedule a backup sitter as a contingency plan.

_____ 12. If your ceremony and/or reception are outdoors at home, don't water your lawn (go ahead and water your flowers) for two days before the wedding. Not watering will minimize muddy spots; slow the growth of grass after your final mowing; and help prevent tent stakes, chairs, and high heels of guests from sinking into the soft dirt.

_____ 13. If your ceremony and/or reception is at home, mow the lawn the day before the wedding (or schedule a service to do so).

_____ 14. Visit a cosmetics counter and purchase permanent lipstick. If you blot and powder between applications, your lipstick will last through the ceremony and photographs.

_____ 15. Buy an antiperspirant and start using it, if you usually only use deodorant. To be most effective, an antiperspirant needs to be used repeatedly for several days.

_____ 16. Arrange for a friend or two to help you and your children dress on your wedding day.

The week before your wedding

_____ 1. Give yourself a break from writing thank-you notes, but *do* continue to write who gave what in your notebook and on your cards, so you can catch up later.

_____ 2. If you will be dressing away from home, gather everything together that you'll need to bring: the gown, veil, lingerie, stockings, shoes, handbag, cosmetics, hairbrush, and so on. Ask your mother or your maid of honor to look everything over to be sure you didn't leave out something vital. Then, do the same for the children. Your groom should be doing this, too.

_____ 3. Pack an emergency wedding-day kit and ask your maid of honor, mother, or best friend to carry it: shoelaces for the children, aspirin, antacid, nail file, spare pantyhose, nail polish, nail polish remover, extra earring backs, tweezers, cosmetics, safety pins, straight pins, sewing kit, antiperspirant.

_____ 4. Have a logistics meeting at home. Review with the troops (you, your groom, your children, and your helpers) where you are meeting (home?), where you'll be moving to (church? hotel?), where you'll be moving on to from there (reception site?), and who will be driving whom. Assign young children to drivers they know and trust, or you run the risk of a screaming 3-year-old interrupting your departure.

_____ 5. Make a list of what's happening for the rest of the week. Stick it on the refrigerator with magnets. This list can cut down the number of times you have to answer questions that begin "Mom, what about...?" It can also help your family visualize and prepare for what's ahead.

_____ 6. Stock up on easy-to-access and nutritious snacks and drinks for the children and houseguests during the week of your wedding.

_____ 7. Buy quiet and entertaining toys and activities to keep your children busy during your wedding rehearsal, wedding, and reception.

_____ 8. If you're taking a honeymoon, review with your children all the details of where they'll be and what they'll be doing.

_____ 9. Does you father look bored? Put him in charge of making sure all the cars are filled with gasoline, have had their oil changed, have tires filled to capacity, and have been through the car wash recently.

_____ 10. Involve your older children with tasks and errands they enjoy: bringing home take-out food for the family, taking younger children out to a movie, arranging the gifts at home, unwrapping presents, and the like.

_____ 11. Pack for the honeymoon. Include your wedding gift for your husband, or if you wish to give it to him before your wedding, arrange a romantic time to do so.

_____ 12. If your children are spending your honeymoon somewhere other than home, pack for them.

_____ 13. Pack your going-away handbag now. Your wedding handbag need only include a handkerchief and touch-up cosmetics. Put other essentials—your driver's license, sunglasses, medications, credit cards, wallet—in your going-away handbag. Ask your maid of honor to take this bag on your wedding day for safekeeping until you are ready to leave your reception.

_____ 14. Have a spa day (which you should have scheduled weeks ago): massage, facial, pedicure, manicure.

_____ 15. Take your children for haircuts. Clip their fingernails while you're at it.

_____ 16. Create a logistics plan for the bathroom. Who takes showers when? Make sure each child has a shower before the wedding.

_____ 17. Polish everyone's shoes. (This is a great job for a child or a grandparent.)

_____ 18. You'll be hungry on your wedding day. Cook ahead or, better yet, arrange for a friend to bring over lunch for you and your children. Order extra food for photographers and others, especially if your ceremony is at home and there will be lots of extra people around.

_____ 19. Make a chronological chart of your wedding day and post it where everyone in the family can see it. Plan extra time for everything. Make a chart for each child, so he or she can manage the day successfully.

_____ 20. If you have a big gown and will dress at home and drive to the ceremony, send someone to the store to buy several packages of white tissue paper. On your wedding day, line your seat in the car with the tissue paper to protect your dress. If you have a train, sit in the front seat and lift your train up and over to the backseat (also lined with tissue paper). If you are dressing at the hotel or church, appoint someone with an empty backseat to drive your gown there. If you wait until the last minute, your gown may travel scrunched into a car with four passengers.

The day before your wedding

_____ 1. Put your honeymoon luggage in the car you'll be taking from the reception to the hotel or airport.

_____ 2. Lay out your children's wedding clothes (but not in a place where they can get soiled or wrinkled).

_____ 3. Gather your wedding clothes in one place, so you won't have to search for anything tomorrow.

_____ 4. Have a special lunch or dinner with your groom—

it's your last chance for a date before you become
an old married couple!

_____ 5. Enjoy visiting with friends and relatives who are in
town for your wedding.

_____ 6. Take a deep breath. You've planned carefully and
thoroughly. Now, you can just enjoy.

The day of your wedding

_____ 1. Take a long, luxurious bubble bath and don't rush.

_____ 2. Use antiperspirant.

_____ 3. Allow lots of time to do your makeup and use a
light touch. This is not the day to experiment with
purple eyeliner.

_____ 4. Give yourself lots of time to dress. Suddenly dis-
covering that all those little buttons on the back of
your gown take five minutes each to fasten can
wreak havoc with a schedule.

_____ 5. Relax. Your time chart gives you and everyone an
easy schedule to follow, so you can all avoid rushing
and feel relaxed.

_____ 6. Spend a loving moment with each of your children
and stepchildren.

_____ 7. During your wedding and your reception, look
around the room and notice all the friends and family who want to share their lives and love with you.
This is where you can find the support and help you
need to create your new family and your new life.

_____ 8. Enjoy your wedding! Congratulations!

After your wedding

____ 1. Check through your notebook or file cards and send thank-you notes to any gift givers who you missed.

____ 2. If you've changed your name, change your driver's license.

____ 3. Change the beneficiaries on your life insurance policy. Make a will (especially important if you have complex custody agreements).

____ 4. Send a thank-you love note to each of your children and new stepchildren through the mail with a real stamp. Name something each child did at the wedding or reception that especially touched you. Kids love getting mail, and your new family machinery can use all the loving "grease" it can get!

____ 5. Enjoy your new life together and appreciate your second chance at love!

INDEX

divorced parents and other
tricky problems, 66–68

drawing up guest list, 64–68

gifts from guests, keeping track
of, 65

invitation to wedding ceremony
but not reception, 63–64

number of guests to invite, 62

out-of-town guests,
accommodations for, 63

seating of, 106

H

Home Depot, 91

Home receptions, 166–67

Home weddings, 96

Honeymoons, 254–61

budget stretchers, 256

budget worksheet, 257

children of wedding couple and,
255, 258, 260–61

choosing a destination, 254,
256

clothing and lingerie for, 258

delayed honeymoons, 255

packing for, 258–59

previous honeymoon sites,
avoidance of, 254–55

staying in touch while away,
261

Hotel weddings, 95

Houseofbianchi.com, 249

Housing arrangements after
wedding, 82–84

announcements about, 131

Humor, 5–6

I

In-laws from previous marriages,
14–15, 16, 22

Interfaith ceremonies, 98–99

Internet, 90–91, 231, 249

Invitations, 122–36

addressing rules, 135–36

at home cards, 130–31

"Black tie invited" notices, 126

when both sets of parents host
the wedding, 127

when bride's mother is
divorced, 126

when bride's mother is
remarried, 127

when bride's mother is
widowed, 126

when bride's parents and
stepparents jointly host the
wedding, 127

for children of wedding couple,
134

extra enclosures, 132–33

formal and classic, 125

freestyle, 128–29

gift-related information, 87,
130

informal handwritten notes,
128

inner and outer envelopes,
133–34

issuing of, 123–24

kid friendly, 129

"No children allowed" notices,
133

for non-church weddings, 125

"No smoking" notices, 128